THE ROCK

THE ROCK

Motivational Leadership:
A Leader's Perspective on Inspiring Others
While Finding the Motivator in You

MILFORD H. BEAGLE JR.

iUniverse, Inc.
Bloomington

The Rock
Motivational Leadership: A Leader's Perspective
on Inspiring Others While Finding the Motivator in You

Copyright © 2012 by Milford H. Beagle Jr..

All rights reserved. No part of this book may be used or reproduced by any means, graphic, electronic, or mechanical, including photocopying, recording, taping or by any information storage retrieval system without the written permission of the publisher except in the case of brief quotations embodied in critical articles and reviews.

iUniverse books may be ordered through booksellers or by contacting:

iUniverse
1663 Liberty Drive
Bloomington, IN 47403
www.iuniverse.com
1-800-Authors (1-800-288-4677)

Because of the dynamic nature of the Internet, any web addresses or links contained in this book may have changed since publication and may no longer be valid. The views expressed in this work are solely those of the author and do not necessarily reflect the views of the publisher, and the publisher hereby disclaims any responsibility for them.

Any people depicted in stock imagery provided by Thinkstock are models, and such images are being used for illustrative purposes only.
Certain stock imagery © Thinkstock.

ISBN: 978-1-4759-4340-5 (sc)
ISBN: 978-1-4759-4341-2 (ebk)

Printed in the United States of America

iUniverse rev. date: 08/07/2012

TABLE OF CONTENTS

Introduction: Words Have Tremendous Power xi

Chapter 1—The Rock 1
Chapter 2—Motivation 9
Chapter 3—Motivation is a Moving Target 18
Chapter 4—Self-Motivation 24
Chapter 5—"G-Notes" 30
Chapter 6—Group Motivation 37
Chapter 7—Distributed Motivation 45
Chapter 8—Drive 52
Chapter 9—Investing 59
Chapter 10—Dream Big 68
Chapter 11—Fun 76
Chapter 12—Me Time 83
Chapter 13—Humility 89
Chapter 14—Listen 95
Chapter 15—Complaining 104
Chapter 16—Change 114
Chapter 17—Confidence 119

Words to Remember: Manchu Quotes 129
Acknowledgements 133
Notes 135

DEDICATION

This book is dedicated to my wonderful family: my wife Pam and two sons, Jordan and Jayden. They are my continual sources of pride, joy, and motivation. I want to thank them for always being there for me and being so understanding through all the ups and downs. You guys are the greatest.

In a time of war, I would also like to dedicate this to those soldiers, Sailors, Airmen and Marines who have made the ultimate sacrifice in the defense of our great nation. Thank you.

FOREWORD

A native of Enore, South Carolina, Army COL Milford H. Beagle, Jr. (Beags) is a down to earth inspirational leader, combat tested officer, and an all around thoughtful Soldier. Having had the privilege of knowing him now for more than 14 years, and serving with him as his battalion commander when he was one of my company commanders, his essay and reflections on the value and strength of motivation in Army organizations captures his thoughtful leadership style and offers "pebbles" of valuable lessons learned that are applicable for not only leaders, but for the led as well; whether in a military or a civilian organization. Imbued with a sense of humor, humility, and self-motivation, Beags has a passion for instilling confidence in one's ability to accomplish any task. He represents the epitome and model of what the Army defines as an inspirational leader. I saw these traits in him early on as a young Captain in the late 90s.

COL Beagle shares his perspectives and experiences on the significance of motivation through 17 chapters of recollections laced with professional insight, reflection, humor, and humility. This work is a valuable treatise on the significance and importance of motivation in organizations; how it creates the will to win, and how the lack of motivation can destroy an organization. Beags' credibility is solid, having served in both Iraq, Afghanistan. Further, he commanded a 1000 Soldier Infantry Battalion in South Korea where he faced the extraordinary responsibility of motivating and leading his unit to accomplish any number of complex individual and collective tasks with the understanding that preparation to fight a war was their most important effort.

As the United States Army faces new challenges in the 21st Century ranging from looming resource constraints to the next combat test, Beags' anecdotes on embracing change, distributed motivation, and determining what drives "you", all serve as useful tools for the reader to use as they consider leading their respective units or organizations. The value of Beags' effort which he succinctly shares in this book is that it is very all personal and told as he has lived—a very special way to share what has worked and what has not worked in his career as a leader of both small and large units.

"The Rock" is worthy of the reader's time and effort to read. I've served our Nation's Army for more than 31 years and have learned as both a commander and staff officer that motivation, humor, and humility often determine the effectiveness of the leadership climate in military units. Beags' effort in this book validates the lessons I've learned in leadership, both in the United States and overseas. He "brings home" the key elements of what it takes to be an inspirational leader.

Major General Michael T. Harrison, Sr.

INTRODUCTION

Words have tremendous power: power to influence, motivate, agitate, bring joy, and the list is endless. The ability to uplift, inspire, and instill hope with the right words, and a genuine concern made a world of difference. Little did I realize the power of my own words as I stood on a large rock looking out at more than 1,000 soldiers.

The rock, large copper and light brownish-colored weighing about 200 pounds with a surface slightly smaller than the average card table, served as a rallying point.

A rally point in military vernacular is a point on the ground where units meet at a predetermined location. There is usually something distinguishable at a rally point—a certain terrain feature or obvious object. Rally points are used for many reasons: to disseminate information, conduct coordination, or as a quick meeting place to make plans for a future operation.

The rock was a predetermined meeting place where coordination was conducted and information disseminated. The information and coordination were not tactical in nature, but motivational.

Every organization needs a rock—not literally, but figuratively. Every organization needs a place where leaders and subordinates can rally to express themselves.

The rally point for the unit gatherings was held in the same location from week to week. During the first few gatherings, it was impossible for me to be seen or heard by the masses. At an above average height of 6'2", it was impossible for me to see or project a loud enough voice for those in formation. Then one day at the usual rally point, I noticed this large rock. Oddly, it was flat and wide enough to stand on, and even pace around, for a few steps without falling off. It was just the right height to stand on and see the entire assembly of soldiers.

This small change made a huge difference. The connection to the soldiers was undeniable because now I could both be seen and heard—more importantly, so could the soldiers. The rock became symbolic of the transformation of our routine gatherings into motivational gatherings. Think of the last meeting you sat in, or for that matter led, and see if you can recall how many times you considered the motivation level of those at the meeting. Inspiring others and motivating groups is often an item that never makes the agenda. The rock allowed me to make inspiration a key agenda item.

The rock removed barriers between the leader and the led. It brought unity to elements of an organization thought to be divided. It helped me reach individuals deemed unreachable. On the face of it, the rock was just an eyesore in the middle of a field, but for 2nd Battalion, 9th Infantry Regiment, it served as a powerful source of motivation.

The following chapters will explain how this inanimate object became the catalyst for transformation and how leaders can incorporate just about anything to inspire others.

The Rock explains my personal views on a component of leadership that I feel is most often overlooked: motivation. It is critical for leaders to incorporate motivation into every aspect of their leadership philosophy. The only definition of leadership that I have gained great comfort and familiarity with over a 22-year military career is the Army's definition. In the Army Leadership Manual, FM 6-22, leadership is defined as the process of influencing people by providing purpose, direction, and motivation while operating to accomplish the mission and improve the organization.[1]

In the framework of this definition, purpose provides the "why" behind the task at hand. Direction helps to put things in perspective by providing general priorities and an overarching order to the task at hand. Motivation is the "fuel" behind sustaining the other two components. Motivation is what makes us tick.

There are scores of great leadership definitions and many do not gravitate far from the principles outlined in the Army's definition. There are several guidelines a leader needs to follow to obtain a high level of motivation: understand people, align and elevate individual goals, learn about others' capabilities and limitations, etc.[2]

The Rock focuses on the motivational aspect of the Army's definition. I believe there has to be a balance between the three components of leadership. An imbalance leads to a semi-dysfunctional organization. I have been a part of high-performance organizations, but morale was extremely low. Individuals knew they had to perform or perish. The motivation was simply to complete one task and move to the next. There was no investment in motivation, only purpose and direction. If big sticks and little carrots serve as your motivational pillars, then *The Rock* is perfect for you. Inspiration and motivation that lasts is not about carrots or sticks. These achieve temporary results at best. What you want are results that carry you or others for a lifetime.

My military experiences can be categorized as typical for a U.S. Army Infantry officer; full of leadership opportunities, managerial experiences, and interactions with practically every culture across the globe.

At age 20, I was in charge of my first platoon (roughly 30 soldiers) and tasked with full responsibility for their mental, physical, and spiritual well-being. This included accountability for several million dollars of equipment. By age 30, I was in command of the second of what would later turn out to be three company-level commands. The Army assigns captains with approximately 8-10 years of experience to a company-level command. Company sizes range anywhere from 75-200 soldiers. In most cases command tenure at this level occurs once and usually lasts for a period of 12-18 months. By exception, some captains may be offered a second command, and he or she may be offered a third command in extremely rare cases. I was both fortunate and blessed to fall into the latter category.

By the time I was 40, the Army had provided me with a series of professional military educational opportunities, key developmental experiences on multiple staffs, and deployments around the world. I am thankful to have earned multiple master's degrees and other military related skills, defended my country in places like Iraq, Afghanistan, and Korea, and have had the privilege to lead soldiers. To date, my experience captures 22 years of military service.

Every leader has a story, and I will share my experiences as an organizational leader in the United States Army. Each of my experiences has been more professionally fulfilling than the last. It was my last leadership experience from 2008-2010, as the battalion commander for the 2nd Battalion, 9th Infantry Regiment (Manchus) forward deployed in the Republic of Korea, that allowed me to further advance my understanding of leadership.

A battalion-level unit is a mid-level command typically reserved for lieutenant colonels with roughly 18-20 years of experience. In most cases, you are selected by a central selection board based on your previous job performance, requisite skills, and match for the position. The unit size ranges anywhere from 500-1,000 soldiers. Organizations of this scale are complex, filled with daily leadership challenges, and contain a wide variety of individual personalities. An organization this size makes it challenging to affect every individual in a meaningful way. What is even more difficult is to motivate an entire organization of this size, get the very best out of each individual, and ignite a level of self-motivation that will carry individuals through a successful career of their own.

Leadership to me is like a marriage; it is a work in progress. Whenever you think you have it figured out, something changes. Once you stop adapting your leadership to those changes, you have stopped leading. Similarly, with a marriage, if you stop adapting to your spouse, the end result is divorce. The last thing a leader wants to do is divorce him or herself from those they lead.

The Rock takes you on a journey down the aisles of motivational leadership from the perspective of leading a complex military organization. Each chapter begins with "pebbles." These little pebbles will help you build your own foundation to stand on—much like the rock—and help you develop or refine your own leadership style—one that emphasizes motivation.

Leaders cannot inspire others if they themselves are not motivated. *The Rock* shares the many tools that I use to inspire individuals as a part of a greater leadership philosophy. Most notable, a big rock, 3 x 5 note cards, personal interaction, and social media.

A military service member, leader of any organization, or a general reader desiring to brush up on leadership, is the intended audience of *The Rock*. Leaders come in all shapes and sizes and lead organizations that vary in the same way. Leaders are faced daily with managerial, financial, personal, and a host of other dilemmas. The one commonality is the objective of getting those within the organization to accomplish a mission over a given period of time in a unified and purpose-driven way. *The Rock* is applicable to the manager who leads a force of one, or the CEO who leads a group of 500, to the military leader who leads thousands.

As you walk away from *The Rock*, my hope is that you realize that motivation begins from within and grows during a constant process of understanding yourself, realizing the conditions or environment around you, figuring out where you want to go in life, and then restarting the cycle all over again. You must always assess and reassess your personal level of motivation.

You are your best cheerleader. Purpose, direction, and motivation apply just as much to you as it does to an entire organization. Organizational leaders can easily provide purpose and direction; the more difficult challenge is to understand how to motivate, how much energy to invest in motivating, and/or having the genuine desire to do it on a consistent basis. Getting it all right, all wrong, and a little in between is a challenge any organizational leader may struggle with. The goal is to achieve a balance between the things that directly impact mission accomplishment and improve the organization.

This can apply to any organization and leaders at all echelons. If you cannot motivate a team of two or a team of 200, you will eventually find your organization at a standstill. If this occurs, your only hope will be to pray that it doesn't slide into the pit of unproductivity, lack of innovation, dysfunction, and worse yet, lack of morale.

An Army Training and Leader Development Program (ATDLP) study identified several interpersonal skills necessary for leaders to be effective within their organizational structures. Of the skills identified by the participants in the survey, 10 were related to interpersonal skills. In rank order beginning with the most important, the skills identified were: providing guidance and direction; motivating and inspiring; fostering commitment; conveying information; mentoring; providing subordinate feedback; teambuilding; listening; persuading; and conflict resolution.[3]

The ATDLP study and many like it raise a serious issue about leadership—interpersonal skills matter. Leaders who relate to their subordinates stand a better chance of success in the long run.

The Rock will help you realize a higher level of personal motivation, provide a lens to discover the motivator in you, and provide a way to inspire others around you.

Recognize the level of motivation within and around you. Observe how your impact affects others. Challenge the cause(s) and challenge the assumptions. Keep a promise to yourself and others to inspire and motivate. R.O.C.K!

Chapter 1

THE ROCK

The rain came down, the streams rose, and the winds blew and beat against that house; yet it did not fall, because it had its foundation on the rock. *Matthew 7:25*[4]

Believe, Buy-in, Build

One thousand men and women stood in formation prepared to listen to another boring brief. I was the one who had to deliver the brief. This brief and every one that followed needed to be different. I needed to inspire and ignite their morale. It was going to launch a turnaround. A new beginning. But how did we get here? What was the tipping point?

For the better part of six months in my tour as a battalion commander, my end-of-the-week "close out" briefs were generally typical. However, the tipping point came when I recognized a few of my senior leaders served as a drain on morale for the entire unit. Although these particular leaders were in part responsible for assisting me as gate-keepers for troop morale, training, and soldier well-being, they were failing.

All leaders desire to have a healthy command climate, an environment that is conducive to work productivity along with individuals who possess a high level of energy and motivation. They were doing everything but fulfilling these tasks.

In order to get an organization to a high performing level, you must work diligently to inspire individuals, set the right example as a leader, and continuously reinforce positive messages and behaviors. When few in the "upper level" management do not express or exhibit these ideals, counterbalancing those negative impacts becomes a full-time endeavor.

I inherently recognized that my unit and organization were doomed for failure. I had to connect with the existing level of motivation and embark on a campaign to inspire as many individuals as possible. It would be hard to overcome the imbalance, but it would not be impossible.

I always sought to maintain a high level of motivation in my organization but now it became my top priority. Morale was not yet at an all-time low nor was the organization completely dysfunctional. In fact, the unit performed very well and there were motivated individuals. However, there were indications that this would become more and more difficult to sustain if left, unchecked, to the negative forces in the organization.

I had to choose the "hard right over the easy wrong." The hard right of fixing the problem at any cost became the solution.

Now just for a second, apply this to your work environment. How easy would it be for some in your organization to emulate the actions of the lazy person, the minimum achieving boss, or to just go with the flow of an existing average level of morale in the organization? If one person is complaining, chances are, others are complaining as well. Mediocrity breeds mediocrity, and once you reach a point at which being mediocre wins, it will be a tough task to reestablish balance.

I identified the problem, now I needed to define the goal and choose the path that would produce the best results.

Every leader wants individuals to be internally inspired. A leader must empower individuals to contribute to the greater good of a larger organization and at the same time realize their self-worth, their strengths, and the value of their individual contributions to the team.

I began by zeroing in on the few individuals in the organization who I felt were the negative force. This is obviously a hard right versus an easy wrong. We have many great tools in the military that are used in order to assist us with dealing with personnel challenges, the foremost being counseling of various natures and types. The use of multiple options is prudent in order to avoid the ultimate decision of having to dismiss or fire individuals. However, firing people is an unfortunate reality that leaders have to be prepared to execute. Former Chairman, Joint Chiefs of Staff, Gen. Colin Powell stressed the consequences of not making a tough decision of this nature. "If you don't fire people who are not doing the job after you have counseled them, after you have brought them along, then you're hurting the whole organization."[5] When initial means were exhausted, I had to develop more creative methods before reverting to mass firings.

First, I decided to conduct my speech at "above ground level." With a formation of more than 1,000 soldiers standing before me, there was no way to look everyone in the eye except by elevating myself above the crowd. I needed them to see me and I needed to see them-from the first rank all the way to the last one in formation. I needed to speak "to" these individuals by speaking "through" the formation. This was how the rock came into the picture. There was nothing special about the rock; it simply elevated me one to two feet above the crowd. With a formation this large, there is no way to look everyone in the eye except by being above the crowd. I had to win over soldiers to my side of the "motivational fence." This may sound like an odd start, but when you are desperate, anything seems like a good idea at the time.

My initial message was not focused on the group; it was intended for the counterproductive individuals. In a loud and commanding voice, I relayed messages and themes that targeted the counterproductive individuals. This was in hopes that maybe the words would resonate in their minds and just maybe, they would start to mimic or even internalize some of the words. For example, I would relay messages about the desire to be a part of a team, doing the right things, dedication to the team and things along those lines.

At the end of these speeches, I would lead the unit in unison by "sounding off" (yell loudly) with our unit name: Manchu. I believed that the louder it was yelled by each soldier, the more they would believe in themselves and the organization. Remember, when you are desperate, you will use any means necessary to begin a turnaround. Sounds like a silly idea now, but at the moment and actually on a whim, it was all I could think of to end my lesson about being a productive member of the organization. It would start by me saying, "We are," and in unison the soldiers would respond with, "MANCHU!" Could you imagine all the employees of your organization saying your unit name with pride in unison? It is an amazing thing! Do not get me wrong; it didn't start off initially as this amazing thing.

I guess you are wondering: What is so special or unique about this, right? Well, initially nothing, because the soldiers had to do it because they were directed. However, over time there were visible results to accompany the pride that I was trying to instill in the unit, but more importantly, the individuals of the unit.

We have an acronym in the Army termed "FEBA". In doctrinal terms it stands for the Forward Edge of the Battle Area. With regard to motivation, it stands for False Enthusiasm and B.S. Attitude! For the first few weeks of this short fiery speech followed by the pep rally-style chant, I could sense a lot of FEBA in the formation. Many simply weren't buying what I was selling and couldn't make the connection. For my part, I had conjured up this plan and by God I was committed to sticking to it.

Next, the use of rewards played an important role in fueling motivation and individual buy-in. As a leader, you have to seek out those who are buying into your vision. Reward those who are aligning with your vision and that of your organization. Let it be well-known that positive individual efforts are appreciated. Always reward in public and reprimand in private. When others see an individual awarded for good things, it is only natural that they will also want their piece of the pie.

Those who had done great things during the week were rewarded during these weekly formations. Nominations were submitted from the subordinate units, in most cases, peers recommending peers and leaders recommending their subordinates. There is no higher honor than to have a peer or your boss recommend you for public recognition. This technique is echoed by Nate Allen and Tony Burgess in their book, *Taking the Guidon,*: "We believe strongly that words, ribbon, paper, or time off is of negligible costs when compared with the results that they often inspire."[6]

Based on Army standards, these awards were not of the official nature. They were unit generated and in many cases simple tokens, but the key was that they were powerful tokens of recognition. So much so that over time there were so many great things happening and recommendations being submitted that it was becoming difficult to recognize the good acts and positive accomplishments in one end-of-the-week formation. I sensed individuals were beginning to buy-in to my messages. They were inspired to do the right thing and in turn, this inspiration was gaining momentum throughout the organization. This may be a hard task to accomplish depending on the type or size of the organization you lead, but whatever the size, you have to start somewhere. Starting by talking with the people of the organization is as good a place as any. If you have to start by talking "at" them or "to" them, simply start by communicating with your people.

As time passed, my messages began to focus on not just the negative individuals, but the unit as a whole. I had their attention, now I had to sustain the momentum and get others around me to help. I exhibited a hands-on approach. My solders needed to know I had a vested interest in their well-being. I could easily get a sense of the unit from day-to-day just by going around talking to soldiers. This is termed "keeping a pulse" of the unit. There are others in the Army who have either specified or implied tasks to assist in this effort (the senior non-commissioned officer, chaplain, and others). The best sources are the soldiers themselves. Similarly, a floor manager can achieve this by walking the work floor from time to time; it is simply talking to people and letting them tell you what is on their mind, good, bad, or indifferent. If I obtained a positive pulse for the week, I would seize upon that.

If there was a negative vibe around the unit, I would seize upon that as well. How? Simply by integrating a message that reinforced the positive or combated the negative, but it always seemed to be the way in which we said our unit name in unison that reinforced the point. Over time, there was pride in saying our unit name simply because we believed in it and what it stood for, individuals believed in themselves and each other. You can tell a championship-caliber team when they take the field or court; they want everybody to know it. I wanted everyone to know that we were a championship team and I wanted them to believe it. Regardless if you have a penguin as a unit mascot or a company name like FedEx, it is not as much about the name as it is about what it stands for, what you want it to stand for, and the principles behind it.

Military units have an advantage because history and a lineage exist for every unit. For a typical business organization, this may be a little harder to establish. Then again, you may have an organization where numbers or dollar figures are the key thing to rally behind, but it would be kind of silly to get everyone to yell and scream about reaching the top dollar figure for the month. My point is to get them to rally around something for starters and build from that point.

Individuals join organizations (especially military organizations) to be a part of something larger than them, a team! Maintaining a high level of team motivation makes it easier to sustain individual motivation. Individuals are easily distracted and thrown off course because of self-doubt or other underlying factors. It is the leader's responsibility to minimize these negative attitudes. It is easy to corrupt the system when motivation is already at a low point.

In *Toxic People*, Marsha Petrie Sue acknowledges this reality of negativity in our daily lives: "You are contaminated every day with toxic infections derived from people, jobs, or your environment."[7] A leader must inspire individuals to develop immunity to these "infections" on their own accord and as a result become self-reliant and self-motivated because they are inspired.

> **Quote from a Soldier: Brett Rochon,** "Motivation: to provide the will to do what needs to be done. A unit can't survive combat without motivation—Soldiers die! With motivation units and soldiers WILL succeed at whatever their mission is. With motivation soldiers will come home alive because their brothers and sisters had a reason to watch over each other."
>
> **Quote from a Soldier: Larry Sack,** "Motivation: knowing and having full understanding of the objective."
>
> **Quote from a Soldier: Philip Gipson,** "If you never strive for greatness you will never achieve excellence . . ."

Chapter 2

MOTIVATION

Motivation comes from within, but is affected by others' actions and words.

—*FM 6-22 Army Leadership Manual*

So there we were! It was a summer Friday in the Republic of South Korea, where a summer afternoon can bring 100 percent humidity on a 90-degree day. Perspiration pours from your body as if you were standing in a shower. The masses had been assembled! Standing on a large rock, I am surrounded by all of the subordinate units of the battalion; more than 1,000 Soldiers. I could see the eyes of the majority, the top of the heads of a few, but I could feel the presence of them all.

This was a common routine every Friday or prior to a period of more than two consecutive days off. All the taboo activities would be covered in detail, a few jokes thrown here and there, and a few key recognitions of soldiers who had performed in an exceptional manner during the week. In all cases, there were many new soldiers in this formation that may not have had a clue as to what would come next, unless their peers shared it with them. For those who truly did not know, they were in for the shock of their new Army career or new duty station.

Based on the briefs that proceeded, there would be a lengthy pause to provide a deliberate break between what had been said before and what was coming next. Chatter would start at a low level; smiles could be seen on the faces of some, and looks of bewilderment on the faces of others. What is this guy [me] about to do or say?

"WE ARE" and in unison, without pause and without fail, the entire formation (with the exception of those that were new to this ritual) would respond with "MANCHU!" We had just motivated ourselves through a demonstration of words, but this was a temporary week-to-week group occurrence. What organizational leaders should want to achieve is a sustainable state of motivation that lasts much longer, is infectious, and goes far beyond the temporary.

I have never considered myself to be a master motivator. However, I have always prided myself on knowing and understanding people. A weekly ritual known as the "close out" formation is how the idea for this book began. These types of formations are not uncommon across the military. They have different names and purposes, but the idea of leader interaction with the masses of the organization has been a part of military organizations throughout history. I would venture to say that the same is true for many other organizations, but it may vary based on context. In this case the general purpose of the Friday briefs was intended as unit safety briefs. The intent was to inform Soldiers of the dangers lurking in the local area and other things to be aware of in order to remain safe and out of trouble over the weekend or holiday period.

Having stood through numerous briefings of this nature before, the briefer tends to sound like Charlie Brown's teacher; "wah, wah, wah," while the only thing you can think about is what are you going to do over the weekend and when will this briefing ever stop. Typically, the unit commander and senior Non-Commissioned Officer lead the brief in a tag-team fashion. The Non-Commissioned Officer generally lays down the ground rules and the all impending punishments that await those who find their way into trouble over the weekend. The unit commander generally covers an additional point or two along similar lines, as well as a host of other points of general information. If nothing else, one thing is clear during the conclusion of these briefs: do not be the poor soul that gets into trouble over the weekend if that is the intended focus of the brief for the week.

Once it became my turn to lead such briefs, I really wanted to ensure that good information was disseminated, at least half the formation learned something new, and try to eliminate the Charlie Brown teacher effect.

I am sure this was the intent of every leader that has ever given one of these types of briefs. This is a tall order for any unit commander because he or she is the only thing standing between a group of young energetic Soldiers and their well-deserved time off. As a young commander, jokes enabled me to accomplish most of my goals regarding the briefs. If nothing else, the jokes broke up the monotony and I was given a little more attention during my portion of the brief. Depending on the senior Non-Commissioned Officer, he or she didn't need any props to keep soldiers fixated on their words. Fear alone would usually do the trick.

One additional tool that I managed to learn from several of my former leaders was the value of making Soldiers feel good about what they do and what they accomplished during the week. Try to give individuals a sense of self-efficacy. In other words, give them a sense of their worth and value within the organization. It is an art in and of itself to properly relay this message to the Soldiers. If you got it wrong, you simply sounded like you were obligated to say what you were saying. If you genuinely believed in what you were saying, you could see and feel the buy-in. It is a tremendous effect to see Soldiers swell with pride and begin to understand and embrace their purpose. One just needs to tap into something to motivate them to do bigger and better things and ignite their internal drive and self-motivation.

The Army includes motivation as a key precept of its leadership definition. However, the manual does not sufficiently describe what motivation is and what you as a leader are to do in an effort to motivate individuals within your organization to achieve mission success and organization improvement. There are several principles and concepts that I agree with in the Army's definition. The idea that motivation is generated from within is one such idea. This is the common understanding and definition of self-motivation. It is hard to argue with this basic premise.

However, I also believe that motivation is elusive; in other words individual motivation levels rise and fall like the tides of the ocean. You never know when these motivational tides will come and go or how high the next wave will be. Tapping into what motivates a person can go a long way toward personal fulfillment and organizational improvement. Gaining and maintaining the ability to inspire others toward mission success is a worthy pursuit for all leaders.

Based on the premise that motivation is elusive, there are things that you can do to "jump start" a person's motivation. Unless he has a high level of self-motivation that is inspired by something unbeknownst to you, you will have to keep jump starting that person. How many times have you seen players of any sport yelling at each other on the sideline to "come on let's go!" and other chants of that nature? They are trying to motivate each other with their words, but when the other team scores, that motivation goes down only to start the motivational cheers all over again. Why didn't the pregame chants and pep talks last throughout the entire game? For the winning team, you can assume that it did. At any rate, the pep talks and riveting speeches start over again the next week. Words alone are powerful, but to sustain motivation requires many additional tools.

It would be a luxury to have those initial motivational speeches last the entire season, only having to say it once. They never do, and won't, because they are temporary. As described in the Army's explanation of motivation, there are different levels based on the individual and most importantly the fact that it comes from within. The continuation of this concept of motivation generated from within states that it is dependent on the "words and actions of others."[8] In his book on *Small Unit Leadership*, Colonel (ret.) Mike Malone states it simply by saying, "Soldiers can be motivated internally, as well as externally, by a leader."[9] The internal and external nature of motivation, like words and actions, are a powerful combination and once combined can lead to lasting motivation. What if the actions and words of others do not exist or simply cease to exist? When this occurs, there is a source void. There are no actions or words that serve the purpose of motivating individuals in the organization. Once a source void occurs, if the actions and words have become so powerful that individuals no longer need the physical presence of the leader in order for great things to continue to happen, I would argue that those individuals in that organization were inspired. In the military, we also refer to this as a sign of a disciplined unit and this is also true, but what is the source of that discipline? Fear, motivation, reward? The best answer is possibly all of the above.

My argument is that if you inspire individuals in a lasting way, the benefits will be countless: good order, good discipline, and yes high levels of self-motivated people. From here, it would only be a short leap to conclude that self-motivation leads to self-discipline. In his book, *Talent is Never Enough*, John C. Maxwell describes self-discipline as the "ability to do what is right even when you don't feel like doing it."[10] But how do you get there? There are a million and one ways to answer this question. This topic has more than likely been broken down into some scientific solution and I surely could have used it, but when dealing with people, it all boils down to being an art. There are no right or wrong and definitely no silver bullet answers when it comes to this subject.

Individuals are constantly seeking sources of motivation to keep them going from day to day. I have heard the argument time and again about how some people's health and level of joy decline very quickly after they retire from a career. That is unless they find something

The Rock

else in their lives to fill the void. In other words what keeps them going is nothing more than what motivates them. They simply lost their motivation source. It could have been a paycheck, the act of the daily routine of going to work around familiar people and places, or simply doing something that they loved. Then there are others that have it all figured out for themselves and everything appears to be a solid source of motivation. It is not a flash of the obvious that personal levels of self-motivation vary from person to person.

For the person who has a low level or small capacity to self-motivate, it takes a great deal of constant and continual external motivation to keep this person upbeat and moving forward. At the opposite end of the spectrum is the person that requires a small dose of external motivation, if any, to keep moving forward and energized. All of us can use a good dose of motivation on any given day. Multiple sources abound all around us, our kids, parents, friends, a pastor, etc. The problem with these physical sources is that they may not always be around, especially when you need them. In either case, motivation sources have to be around and available on a consistent basis in order to provide the extra boost that some of us need at any given time. This is never the case, right?

This is where relying on inspiring individuals toward self-motivation becomes key. It has always been engrained in Army leaders that self-discipline is doing the right thing even when no one is watching. In order to be disciplined, you have to be self-motivated. In order to be self-motivated, you must have that internal inspiration—that one thing that drives you forward. That one thought, that one goal, or the thought of that person(s) that will keep you focused, and yes motivated! If you are internally inspired by someone or something, chances are you are always pretty self-motivated. Sure, the source may change from time to time, but you always need to have an ignition source. The goal is always to motivate, but I argue that there is far more benefit to be gained when you seek to inspire. I can motivate you for 10 minutes with a fiery speech standing on a rock or inspire you for a lifetime by believing in what I am saying, believing in you and demonstrating it on a daily basis as a leader. The eventual goal is getting you to share the same level of enthusiasm. This is when motivation turns to inspiration and individuals have a self-sustaining method to achieve the unachievable, to believe the once thought unbelievable and sustain a determination that will endure.

In all cases I viewed the fiery speeches from the rock as their commander temporary, but based on my actions and those of others, Soldiers became inspired. It is flattering that new-found levels of motivation are attributed to you, but the credit belongs to the Soldier. It takes a personal desire to allow external things to affect you mentally. By welcoming this external source, individuals were in effect motivating themselves.

> **Quote from a Soldier: Billy Wright**, "Motivation is what divides a soldier who doesn't quit from a person who thinks his limit is based on his comfortability. The reason why soldiers do 25-mile ruck marches for a belt buckle and a coin."
>
> **Quote from a Soldier: Stan Stewart**, "I am always motivated!"

Quote from a Soldier: Erik Choquette, "Anytime I feel like giving up I think, *Is this how you are going to die?* because to me that's what you are doing when you give up; you are witnessing your own death."

Chapter 3

MOTIVATION IS A MOVING TARGET

Pebbles: As long as you never quit . . . you will never be counted out!

If you have ever fired a weapon where acquiring and engaging a moving target is involved, you will know that it is no easy task. Often, it is difficult to select the correct time and point to fire in order to hit a moving target. Motivation is somewhat similar; it can be elusive, sometimes hard to acquire, and at times difficult to attain. Oftentimes, you can never truly pinpoint the one thing that motivates you from day to day. Some days you feel so alive and full of energy—motivated! Then there are other days where you simply do not want to get out of bed—unmotivated! When you experience the latter, your goal is to acquire and attain the motivation you lost. But how?

To successfully shoot a moving target, you must lead the target. It is a simple math problem of speed and trajectory. Targets moving at a given speed in a certain direction will require the shooter to aim in front of the target (lead) in order for the speed of the bullet to compensate for the distance of travel.

If you aim at the moving target, you are essentially chasing the target. Once the trigger is pulled, the target continues to move along its path. It took the bullet too long to travel the given distance. The opportunity was missed! However, a little forward thinking and getting ahead of the problem allows one to lead the target. The critical point to focus on in this analogy: lead the target. When you are chasing the motivation that you had yesterday, or two weeks ago, you are doing just that, chasing it! In order to get it back, you want to "lead" your current state of motivation. Get ahead of what is affecting you. Find that point ahead of this lull in motivation so that you can intersect it and eliminate this most dangerous threat to your daily life—low motivation.

No matter the situation or feeling of doom—bad day at work, bad relationship, or just experiencing a bad week; you want to get ahead of it. This is where lead comes into play. Think of the things you look forward to or want to look forward to. There is something out there for all of us to look forward to. If there is not, try to do your best to do something about it. Of course, this is easier said than done. You can't just drop your current job if you are having a bad work experience on a daily basis. However, you can focus on things to shape the conditions to get a better job. This now becomes your motivating factor; this is applying that "lead." This becomes your new focus. The excitement of searching for a new job or taking classes that you know will lead eventually to getting the job you really want. I never said that there were easy solutions to getting ahead of the source of your motivation problems. The key task is to get ahead of it.

The other implied task of getting ahead is to figure out how much of a lead you really need. You don't necessarily have to have a substantial lead time. Like the shooting example, the amount of lead required in order to hit a target all depends on how fast the target is moving and how far away you are from that target. How close is this impending low motivation to you? Is it a constant thing? Or is it a semi-regular thing; high one week and rock bottom the next? Only you know the answer to this, but whatever the answer is, you will have to determine the amount of lead that you need. If your source of low motivation comes around infrequently, such as when the top-level boss comes to visit once a month, focus on the day after that one point of the month. Think about how happy you will be tomorrow when he or she will not be around.

If have low motivation every day, like the moment you walk into the office, you will have to be pretty innovative to get through this dilemma. For starters, you could focus on those things you do well. Focus on your ability to help others. Part of what motivates us, is the joy we find in helping others. We tend to like ourselves and view ourselves in a positive way due to the good feeling we get from helping others. Think of the last time you did a good deed. How did it make you feel? Establish a lead by focusing on someone else. Helping others usually makes us happy and the one person that you want to be happiest is, of course, you.

You may think that this sounds a bit selfish, but trying to make the boss or others happy all the time at the expense of your own personal happiness is a recipe for disaster. Contributing as much as you can to the best of your ability serves two purposes: On the one hand, you are doing something that is self-fulfilling and on the other hand, you are maximizing your contribution to the team. You have to successfully keep your aim point ahead of the target and when you finally pull the trigger...target down! You win by not allowing the negative forces to ruin your day. The victory belongs to you and by extension—your team, your organization.

Conversely, you may sometimes find yourself so immersed in getting ahead of things that constant worry and stress are the end result. If we look at the "lead" principle of engaging targets, we can apply this analogy in a different way. At the time an expert shooter is engaging that moving target, time stands still for an instant. Breathing stops, vision becomes solely focused on the target, the heart rate slows, and senses are aroused to the point of excitement; then bang! The target goes down.

During personal times of low motivation or self-induced high stress, the focus must be along the same lines. Slow the things around you down; eliminate the distractions and noise. Focus on the one thing that is serving to drag on your morale; this is now your target. So what do you do next? There are many options depending on what the cause is, but like the shooter, you must first clearly see your target, focus, and reduce the stress of other things going on around you. For example, let us say that the cause is another person. Chances are you are not going to change that person just as the shooter can't slow the progression of a moving target. However, you can change yourself. Where is the next point you want to be? What is the next goal that you want to achieve? The answer is now your lead. The goal is now to prevent the other person from distracting you from your new aim point. Once you commit yourself to engaging, you have now set your conditions for success and new-found motivation. Hopefully you will now be able to sustain your motivation based on finding this new point to aim.

Many times I would see soldiers who could not find an aim point. They would become distracted by the moment or source of their frustration. They would carry these thoughts and frustrations to the next day, then the next, and so on. Unlike the shooter, they couldn't find that point of excitement. Everything was a tangled mess and hopelessness became their new best friend. They became carried away in the whirlwind of everything but the target at hand. As a result, their own motivation became the victim.

A brief example, I encountered a soldier who was simply miserable. No one in his chain could figure out why he was so unmotivated and miserable. I spoke to him and he relayed to me that he simply wanted out of the Army. When I asked how long he had been in the unit, his response was "three weeks." When I asked how long his obligation was, he replied "four years." I kind of laughed and said, "You have a long way to go and even longer if you are going to remain miserable." What he really wanted was an opportunity to go to college. He joined the Army in hopes of achieving a better life, but found himself miserable. He didn't like the unit, the location, or his current station in life. When I asked had he done anything to pursue classes, etc., he informed me that he had not. He had no aim point and hadn't applied any of his energy to his real goal in life; this is what was making him so miserable. It really wasn't the unit, or the people, or other. It was him.

I recommended that he check into the class offerings at the education center and directed that he go there. A week later, he had signed up for some classes. I began to notice that he smiled more and was more interactive with his fellow soldiers. Two years later, he informed me that he was accepted to a local college in his hometown. He was so inspired that once he applied his "lead" and focused on his true goal, he became a better contributor all around. The little things that use to bother him didn't, and the frustration that he felt daily had all but subsided.

At last, he was motivated and proud of what he had done, but the effort was all his. He possessed the motivation all along, but he didn't know how to channel it. He was afraid to pull the trigger of his own motivational weapon.

> **Quote from a Soldier: Rob Rollins,** "You can't judge a man by his past, but what he does with his future."
>
> **Quote from a Soldier: Scott Afonso,** "Anything in life that is worth having is worth sacrificing something for . . . If you're not willing to sacrifice then don't complain and take that which others have sacrificed for."

Chapter 4

SELF-MOTIVATION

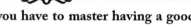

Pebbles: To be good you have to master having a good day even on a bad day.

How often have you gotten out of bed and made some expletive regarding going to work? "I have to F#$%^ go in to see these @$$&^*(@ people again today!" or "!@$% I hate going in to this place!" This obviously makes it hard to start the day off as a good day. No matter what, you have just limited not only yourself, but anything positive that could possibly happen for you that day. I am just as guilty of having done this on occasion; I'm sure we all have at some point or another. However, if this is your daily ritual upon waking, you seriously need to find another job or take another look at what inspires you.

I encounter individuals who make mistakes and they would just chalk it up to: "they just had a bad day." There is a lot of truth in this statement, but my personal belief is that the above-average person could manage to have a good day even on a bad day. How is this possible, you may ask? Simple, don't bring the bad day with you. I am convinced that those individuals who always seem to have things in order and never really seem to have a bad day actually do have bad days, but they simply won't allow it to affect them or others. I would relay to subordinate-level leaders that their peers who were performing better or achieving more than they, had simply mastered not having bad days. At a glance, you may think that some people are just good at masking problems or are really good at pretending problems in their lives don't exist. This may be true to an extent, but eventually those problems will come to the surface no matter how deeply they are suppressed. I firmly believe that there are those individuals who place a great deal of value on the word focus, which in turn allows them to function at a high level even when things around them may not be going so well.

So how does this relate to turning a good day into a bad day? Everything. Have you ever gone to the counter of your local fast food establishment and could instantly tell that the person on the other side of the register was having a bad day? You probably left that experience saying "who licked the red off of their lollipop" or "wow, they should have really stayed at home today." In some cases this serves to put you in a foul mood as well. Your order was not correct; you didn't receive correct change; or you may have even had a heated exchange with the person. At any rate, that person made sure that their problem just became your problem and you allowed it! Negative energy is contagious! I am in no way trying to imply that the person should ignore a problem, because there may be a serious issue on the mind of this individual and a very valid reason behind that person's smile being upside down.

I will come back to this point in a second, but in all professions, it is almost inherent that you have to have good days, day after day. Would you like to go into surgery knowing your surgeon's attitude is not in check or better yet, take the flight with the pilot who has his or her mind in another place? With Soldiers, we consider our occupation one that doesn't take any prisoners or give "do-overs." When you are using real bullets, fighting a real enemy threat, as we are today around the globe, one mistake could be a costly one. Unfortunately, a mistake on your part due to a lack of focus may not bring harm to you, but to someone else. One thing we used to say before we would leave the FOB (Forward Operating Base) for missions is to "leave your bad day behind." In most cases this is easier said than done, but one thing is for sure, you relied heavily on each individual being able to do just that. Why should you or anyone else pay the price or carry the burden of someone else's bad day?

Having the ability to focus and put your best foot forward under even the worst circumstances is a trait worth developing. In the case of not only service members, but with many professions, it could be the difference between life and death. So how do you commit to this level of focus on a consistent basis? Focus on everything except your problem. Help someone else resolve their problem. You have to personally take on the responsibility to contain your problems. This does not mean that you avoid seeking help or solutions. Rather, it is a way for you to focus on keeping the bad behaviors associated with personal problems in check. By containing your problem, you check a negative attitude that leads to negative words, which could lead to negative actions and so on. One thing is for sure, if the problem is big enough, it will still be there when your time on the job is over.

There are many exceptions to this when the problem at hand seems simply too overwhelming to bear. I will say that I have seen some amazing feats of focus from others in my own career and personal life; close relatives passing away, soldiers discovering they or a family member has cancer, or even divorce papers coming in the mail. Despite the pain and mind games that events like this will play on a person, I have seen soldiers perform as they would on any typical day only because they knew someone else was counting on them to do their part. This is a heavy burden to bear. The obligation to uphold their end of the bargain and the fact that others depended on them kept them focused.

This dynamic of obligation and commitment to service is in play for jobs in every occupational field. Whether it occurs in all occupations or not is a different story altogether. At any rate, try to think of one occupation where this dynamic of obligation does not occur. I'll give you a couple for starters, the all-time favorite—ditch digger! Well, what if he or she did not survey the ground properly and dug up your water line? What about a grave digger? Ever seen a grave dug too shallow or narrow and the casket wouldn't fit properly? What an embarrassment at the gravesite and a lack of dignity shown to the family and the deceased. I've seen that before, not a pretty picture. No matter what you do, someone is depending on your million-dollar effort every day. In most cases, "sorry" or "oops my bad" won't lessen the mistake to any degree. We are obligated to each other in some form or fashion whether we like it or not.

The fact that someone is depending on you is motivation enough for some. On the other hand, this is a de-motivator for others. Sometimes people just don't care about others, so why should they feel motivated about anything, not to mention doing a good job? "I can afford to do a crappy job and not really care about the consequences, because it is not my problem." Many of us have possibly heard words to this effect. To prevent these words from coming from you, you must find a source that will allow you to motivate yourself. If you are motivated, you can focus, if you are inspired, you can focus. If not, every day becomes a bad day.

Sure you can't mask every problem that you may encounter on a daily or weekly basis. The goal is to simply learn how to focus on the task at hand because whether you believe it or see it, someone is counting on you to do the right thing. Everyone won't realize that you are having a bad day, and in most cases it is not their obligation to realize it. The alternative is to tell everyone that you encounter: "Hey, today I'm having a bad day. I can't be as helpful to you today as I will be later in the day or tomorrow." Yeah that is the right answer . . . not! It is up to you to control your motivation, attitude, and focus. Others can help you, but it predominately rests on your shoulders. Inspire yourself to make every day a good day. Before long, every day is a good day. When the bad day does come around; it will be hard for others to notice because you have mastered the art of turning bad into good.

Quote from a Soldier: Derek Parnell, "Motivation is what you expect your leaders to do for you in order to accomplish the mission. Self-motivation is the drive you have within that allows you to accomplish ANY mission whether your leaders are present or not."

Quote from a Soldier: Jason Anderson, "I feel the idea of self-motivation is flawed. Just as all humans are self-concerned and self-absorbed, I feel motivation comes from a comparison with others. Therefore, self-motivation comes from competition or wanting to be better than your neighbor."

Chapter 5

"G-NOTES"

Pebbles: "Think through the idea of handwritten notes and if you believe in it, implement it—you will both raise the morale of your organization and surprisingly, you will be rewarded in retirement . . . ."

—retired Colonel Gregory Gardner[11]

I mentioned earlier that I learned many positive ways to inspire from some great leaders. The most memorable was from one of my former commanders; Colonel Greg Gardner. He was, in my view, the master of motivation and individual inspiration. One of the many tools Colonel Gardner used at the time was something we referred to as "G-notes." These notes were always handwritten and generally about a paragraph in length. His signature ending was the circle "G," hence the name "G-note."

As a regimental-level commander, meetings, briefings, and signing the tons of paperwork that came with the territory left him little time for much else. However,

The Rock

Cololonel Gardner was always out and visible among the troops, even if it required 3:00 a.m. visits. What baffled a majority of us the most was his ability to produce "G-notes" on a consistent basis. We knew his time was very limited and action-packed every minute of the day, and to produce these notes with such consistency was absolutely amazing. We never figured out when he had time to write the notes.

The notes would relay how pleased he was with a particular performance or his pride in personally observing a positive accomplishment of a soldier. Having been on the receiving end of a few "G-notes," the power of this simple 3x5 style card with a few words from the boss was amazing. They would make you feel very proud of what you accomplished and leave you with a desire to accomplish more. Not for want of receiving another "G-note," but because you were recognized as a contributor, and your performance was valued. In fact, it was valued so much that the "head man" himself took his personal time (whenever that happened to be) to write you a note. Man! This said a lot about him as a leader and just as much about your actions. I can remember performing room inspections and seeing "G-notes" randomly posted in soldiers' rooms. It was then that the magnitude and power of this simple act struck me. Within an organization of more than 1,200 soldiers, there were probably two out of three soldiers who had received a "G-note." This is profound when you do the math, and did I mention how extremely busy Colonel Gardner was on a daily basis? Everybody knew how busy he was, but he still made the time to pen these notes.

These notes went a long way in terms of inspiring people. Just a glimpse of the note posted wherever you may have posted it, was a constant source of inspiration for the one time that you did something great, and it didn't go unrecognized. You could have done many great things before that, but it was well worth it simply to be recognized once. This allowed you to keep focused on your current azimuth and bolster your own self-motivation. It is simple acts like these that make an average organization better, an uninspired person inspired, and takes a mediocre organization to new levels.

This was surely a tool that I retained in my "kit bag" during my command tenure. It worked just as well for me as it did for Colonel Gardner. I have used it at two levels of command since my first encounter with Colonel Gardner as a young staff officer. The end result was the overarching effect that you wanted to achieve—inspired individuals! You couldn't write a "G-note" for one individual just to keep them motivated from week to week, but if one "G-note" inspired them for the foreseeable future, you had achieved success, in my view. Nothing is more powerful than an individual who is fueled by their own drive and if it only required a small ignition source like a "G-note," then the few minutes it took to write the note was well worth the investment in time. The words of Colonel Gardner did not only motivate, they inspired you to continue doing great things. It was not because someone else expected it from you, but because you now expected it of yourself.

This made a believer out of me that written and spoken words are equally powerful as motivation tools. This may seem like a flash of the obvious, but what truly struck me was their power to create lasting motivation. In the period of observing Colonel Gardner issue G-notes for soldiers in my company-level unit, there were only about one percent who would ever come up for some type of trouble after receiving a note. As for my own experience, the same is true. Only about one percent of the soldiers who I personally wrote a "G-note" to would ever stumble into any future type of trouble. The 99 percent continued to excel. I attribute the cause as being the "G-note." The effect was the pride instilled in the individual thereby empowering him or her to achieve new levels of self-motivation.

Honestly, in some cases, and especially in large organizations, you can easily lose track of whom you had given a "G-note." As a battalion-level commander, I certainly did this on occasion. A Soldier would thank you for a received "G-note" (even though they didn't carry this same name for those that I wrote), and you would quickly have to process the name with the event to reciprocate or elaborate to the Soldier on his or her good performance. A gesture like the "G-note" is not a matter of tracking them or keeping a register of who you sent a note. It is about the thought that went into the note. I learned that it was okay on occasion to forget to whom you had sent a note because what meant most to the recipient was the fact that you took the time. In some cases, you might even receive a return note in kind thanking you. It seems odd to receive a thank you note for a thank you note, but it happens. Your words and actions as a leader go very far in inspiring individuals.

To many of the younger soldiers, just as the case may be for many young employees in any organization, you represent the wisdom of the organization and there are a few individuals who aspire to be like you whether you recognize it or not. A simple thing such as sharing a part of your story may be the boost that motivates and inspires someone to reach higher goals.

I recently had breakfast with "Mr. Gardner" and although he is well into his retirement these days, he continues to keep up his practice of "G-notes." As a key member of NetApp (a large Defense Solutions firm in northern Virginia), his practice of "G-notes" is impacting people there just as they did during his time in the active duty military. NetApp was recently named one of *Washingtonian Magazine's* 50 Great Places to Work.[12] In a short office publication for NetApp titled, "Secrets to Success: Personal is Memorable," Mr. Gardner, outlined some tips for successful personal notes:[13]

1. These are not notes sent on the occasion of birthdays or promotions . . . those have little value.
2. These are notes written to subordinates after you personally witness their performance. This means you have to walk around and, as the old "One Minute Manager" recommended, catch people doing something right.
3. The notes are addressed to and delivered directly to the individual, not through a manager/leader, and should be received by the individual within 24 hours of the behavior mentioned in the note.
4. The notes are uniformly positive and complimentary, though brief. NEVER is there any form of negative comment in any one of these notes.
5. The notes address the individual's specific performance and include a comment about how important that individual is to the organization.

6. The notes are written on a unique card stock and sealed in an envelope addressed to the individual.
7. Notes should be a routine practice. In an organization of 1,500 people, the leader might write between 5-10 each day—again, each based on specifically observed performance.

- A closing note of caution: Before a leader begins writing these notes, she/he must commit to writing them throughout their tenure. If they peter out and stop, the organization will view the practice with cynicism as another flash in the pan leadership fad.

As you can see, a note of this nature would go a long way for an individual's motivation. Although I may not have remembered all of Mr. Gardner's rules, I remembered the overall intent and it has stuck with me ever since. In his short piece written for NetApp, Mr. Gardner captures the overall idea of notes in the following way:

> *We often forget that men and women at all organizational levels have their own significant ambitions, each wants to look forward to coming to work in the morning; each wants to be a winner. It may not seem like a big thing, but I have found that sending handwritten notes to employees when they do something particularly well—or even up to standard—is a very powerful motivator.*[14]

Personalized leadership is important. There is no better way of expressing that than through time, consistency, and genuine effort. Nothing captures these three elements better than a personal note. Inspiring others can take time, but one of the most effective ways to inspire is to devote a little of your time for the benefit of others.

> **Quote from a Soldier: Jason Anderson**, "When I find myself falling on tough times or lacking that spark, I try to remind myself to pause . . . breath, and remind myself of all the important people in my life that are counting on me."

> **Quote from a Soldier: Ken Nagata**, "If you want something that you have never had before, and then you must do something you have never done before." In order to practice this you must have perseverance and guts."

Chapter 6

GROUP MOTIVATION

Pebbles: Being a leader is not only about being out front; it is about focusing on those behind you. Keep them fed with motivation, quench their thirst with pride, and give them genuine concern for desert. The next thing you know, you have a following that will always accomplish the mission.

Motivation can begin anywhere in an organization. It can begin from a bottom-up perspective just as easily as it can begin from a top-down perspective. I think people would be skeptical to believe that organizational motivation is not always linked to a dynamic leader. I have found that group motivation centers on accomplishment of the mission. Given a clear vision and an executable task, groups can accomplish practically anything, and they often generate a high level of motivation in the process. I recognize that this sounds typical coming from a military officer. Oftentimes, one person accomplishing a single mission can go viral and inspire many others to do bigger and better things. This ignites a level of group motivation that started from a single effort. In many cases, leader(s) have to foster an environment where this type of initiative is welcomed, encouraged, and facilitated.

How well an organization accomplishes missions is linked to the level of group motivation. Success in many things breeds confidence and a sense of pride throughout the organization. Easy link right? What about when things are not going so well for the organization? A lot of pressure will befall that leader to keep things on track. He or she will have to dedicate a great deal of energy to finding those things that will give the unit that sense of pride and accomplishment. In most cases, the leader has to start small and work toward achieving larger goals.

In your assessment, if the organization is really in a huge state of disarray, you have to start really small. You must look for those small things that may have big impacts or better yet, seek out the one individual who is constantly doing a good job, but does not necessarily feel or see the rewards. In all cases, you want to connect the dots between individual motivation, group motivation, and a common or shared purpose.

Remember to give credit where credit is due. The person who observed you invest your energy in their project will be sure to now assist you in spreading the wealth around the organization. You produced results for them, which allowed them to produce results for the organization, and they will be sure to let others know. They will feel the pride in their collective sense of worth. Creating an organizational climate that fosters new ideas and encourages initiative increases motivation.

Motivating individuals is one thing, but motivating groups is another. With individuals, you are trying to understand what will motivate them to connect to the larger group. With a group, you are trying to understand what motivates a particular group to connect to the other or larger group(s).

Motivating a group that has its own level of cohesiveness, connection, and in some cases its own culture, is difficult. This motivation can come internally or externally. Ultimately, you want the group to be internally inspired. As the leader, your goal is to set the conditions for allowing the group to internally generate, sustain, and maintain its motivation in relation to the rest of the team.

Gaining and sustaining group motivation from within a group is a tricky endeavor. The first rule is to commit to this endeavor. The second rule is to figure out the group dynamics. Third, figure out the connection between the group and the larger purpose. Group motivation requires an understanding of group dynamics within the organization. What inspires a group to connect to a larger cause is essential to the group's level of motivation. Similar to individuals, groups will connect to a larger cause when it feels its contribution is valued. If a group is perceived or perceives itself as less than a valuable contributor, motivation will likely suffer.

Committing to group motivation is self-explanatory. It takes an iron will and a lot of persistence to achieve this goal. Making everyone happy is not the focus. Finding a balance where there are more happy than disgruntled people is the focus. Understanding group dynamics is essential to overcoming barriers to group motivation and is more difficult to figure out. The cliché of "strong as the weakest link" is important to understanding group motivation. Leaders of any organization have to realize that separate groups within a larger organization are all strong links. More importantly, everyone in the organization has to understand and buy into this "strong link" concept.

On the surface this may appear to minimize contributions of other groups that are perceived as the "workhorses" of the organization. If a leader is not careful, an inability to balance negative perceptions could serve as a point of friction that could un-inspire other parts of the organization. This is why leadership is so difficult. Tough choices and thoughtful decisions are not easy to make. In trying to achieve this balance, the goal is not to inspire one group and deflate another. Motivating groups requires an understanding of how the overall organization works, as well as the relationships of subordinate groups within the organization.

Barriers to group motivation come in the form of stereotypes between groups, negative perceptions of individuals within groups, or disparity in work productivity, etc. As an example, certain Army units have their own cooks. Cooks work long hours, and in most cases they work seven days a week year-round. Soldiers often complain about Army food and regardless of the effort, it will never compare to McDonalds or Burger King. Therefore, Army cooks often feel undervalued for their efforts to provide a quality service; food! However, soldiers often fail to realize that without cooks they don't eat, and when they don't eat, they can't perform their mission. Nevertheless, this does not prevent cooks from being the butt of jokes regarding Army food. This does not manifest itself in a mean-spirited way, but it can be a source of friction when it comes to realizing the total efforts of every group in a unit.

Unlocking group motivation requires ensuring those at the top of the organization understands the dynamics and level of connectivity of groups within the organization. To raise the level of awareness in the organization, separate groups should understand its connection to the larger organization's purpose, mission and its role.

Awareness is critical because leaders and subordinate groups sometimes forget this fundamental principle. When this occurs, the larger organization becomes individual groups operating independently of each other versus operating interdependently. In large or small organizations, interdependency is key to success and motivation.

I will illustrate interdependency in the following example: An Infantry soldier operates at the leading edge in battle. His mission is to close with and destroy his enemy. His primary weapon is a physically fit body and his secondary weapon is his rifle. Sustaining and maintaining this soldier at the leading edge requires a cook who prepares meals. When a hot meal is not feasible, ready-to-eat meals (prepackaged food) must be delivered by a distribution unit. If his rifle breaks beyond the soldier's ability to repair, a maintenance group is required to fix it. If the soldier is hurt or injured, there is a medical group whose mission is to tend to injuries and provide aid.

In military jargon, these groups have names such as squads, platoons, companies, etc. Each has a separate function, but they all work toward a shared mission and common purpose. If any of these links are weak, the entire chain is weak.

Group motivation requires leaders to recognize and make everyone aware of these connections. Leaders must also reinforce the value and importance of each group represented in the chain. If one group is under-inspired and underappreciated, this in turn has a profound effect on their motivation. They may have thoughts like: "*Why are we giving 100 percent effort only to have our efforts go unrecognized?*" Leaders must point out every group's contribution, whether it is direct or indirect, to the larger effort.

Think of it this way, if you feel that your individual contribution is not valued in the group that you are a part of, it is likely that this affects your level of motivation. Your concern is less about the overall mission or purpose of the larger organization. You don't feel valued, so why should you put stock in an effort that doesn't return the favor? This can occur with an entire group just as easily as it can with one individual. Devalue the group and soon they won't put stock in an effort that doesn't put stock in them.

Leaders inspire both by showing the connectedness to a greater good (the mission) and recognizing the value of all involved in contributing to the greater effort. Small contributions are recognized equally with big contributions.

As an example, I, along with thousands of others, read some sort of news during our daily commute on the Washington, D.C. Metrorail system. There are two main papers that are distributed for free each morning, the *Express* and paper "X" (I chose to leave the other newspaper un-named). Both newspapers are distributed by average people, but the *Express* vendors are different. They routinely greet you with "Good morning, would you like an *Express*?" If you don't take their paper, they often tell you, "Have a nice day, sir/ma'am." Every day I read the *Express*, I am delighted to see a picture of one of the vendors with a caption that expresses the newspaper's thanks for doing such a great job.

The caption speaks to the vendor's positive personality and attitude. The vendors are probably not the best paid workers in the greater D.C. area, and I would assume that there are not many perks of the job, but they do it well because they are recognized and appreciated. On the other hand, I have yet to see employee acknowledgements like this in the other paper. From my personal observation, it shows. Each morning, I observe how fast the *Express* stacks disappear while paper X's stack trail in distribution. The employees of paper X don't seem as happy and clearly would rather be doing something else at 5:30 a.m. besides handing out free newspapers.

To me an organization like the *Express* gets it; they get interdependence and connectedness, and it shows. If it weren't for their vendors, their paper would sit in stacks like paper X. The stars of the newspaper team are obviously the writers, editors, printer people, etc., but I have yet to see a picture of them in the newspaper. Besides, I would only assume that they have other ways of recognizing those employees. The point is, the organization is thoughtful enough to recognize the person at the bottom of the chain as being a strong link.

Every person and sub-group is critical to the larger cause of any organization. When a chain that has a weak link is put under stress, it breaks. Every link is critical. The leader's responsibility is to inspect the chain daily and perform preventive maintenance to ensure that no weak links emerge. Group motivation is never this clean or simple, but making the connections and recognizing the value of the groups within the organization will go a long way toward group motivation.

Quote from a Soldier: Vincent Mortara, "Group motivation means that everyone in a group is willing to do what needs to be done FOR THE GROUP. There can be no individuality with group motivation. The focus needs to be on success of the group, not the failure of a few."

Quote from a Soldier: Jason Anderson, "It's when you can take ten people, put them together, and with their commitment and unity to each other get the strength of 20 people."

Quote from a Soldier: Stan Stewart, "The whole group is motivated toward the same goal."

Chapter 7

DISTRIBUTED MOTIVATION

Pebbles: The next time someone tells you to "think outside of the box" (and this happens to be commonplace where you work) . . . Kindly respond with "We probably need a new box!"

Facebook was one of the social networking tools that I had avoided like the plague since its inception. I didn't avoid it out of fear of sharing part of my personal being with the world. For the most part, I avoided it because I felt it was too time-consuming. Due to the various other forms of communication that any organizational leader has to deal with (email accounts, cell phone, web pages, Sharepoint, Blackberry, etc.), adding one more reduced having time for other more important things, so I thought. Little did I know or understand then that this was another avenue to reach out to soldiers. This is not a new or novel idea, but one that I hadn't cared to dedicate much thought.

Unbeknownst to me, this was a key method of soldier communication. Once I decided to give it try, the first danger that I considered was the fact that I would never be able to connect with the soldiers using Facebook. Besides, would you really want your boss as one of your friends? Put up the wrong post on your wall and watch out for trouble; Yikes!

I decided to give it a try and at first didn't really know what to put on my posts. Then I figured that I would simply use it as an extension of my Friday speeches. It provided another opportunity to connect with the individuals who I may not have reached otherwise. Thus, social media provided me with an alternative context for leadership.

Leadership involves the leader, the led, and a context. They interplay with each other like the workings of a well-oiled machine. Social media provided a new and different context. More importantly, I wanted to do my best to use this new-found context to post words of encouragement (Pebbles) on my wall for those who needed a little extra boost.

My friend requests were very slow at first and I immediately attributed it to my earlier comment, respond to your bosses friend request? IGNORE ... NOT NOW! Well I started putting up posts that I thought touched on some of the things that I had witnessed or even discussed with soldiers during the week. What I found was that it is amazing how many times I received a reply that stated, "That is just what I needed to read," or in some cases, "Wish you had posted that yesterday (smile)." I will never claim to be a Dr. Phil or Dear Abby for those who even remember who Dear Abby is. I enjoy being around people, but more so listening to them and their stories. There is much to be learned simply by listening. It was listening to soldiers and their stories that provided me the inspiration to write some of the things that I would post.

Over time, I began to realize that many in my social network circle had committed to positive messaging themselves. This brought me many smiles. People were inspired and I had just witnessed "distributed motivation." To me, distributed motivation is to directly or indirectly influence others in a positive way, resulting in a change to a person's level of motivation. This can be accomplished through direct contact, texting, Facebook posts, or whatever comes to mind. Social media has given us a new box! Motivational "pebbles" were generated by others and passed along. Chalk another one up for the individual who no longer needed a boost. He or she now had enough internal stores of self-motivation to not only sustain themself, but to also embark on the mission to inspire others.

It will always be a work in progress to figure out how to connect with all individuals within your organization. By no means are any options off the table. For me, the Facebook option fell into my lap. Keep in mind that there is no right or wrong answer, but sometimes an answer will be staring you right in the face. I learned a very important lesson about this tool, and it is like many of the lessons associated with my ideas. It simply takes time. I was initially worried about the drain of time that Facebook would require, but I am a firm believer that you will dedicate time to what you feel is important. Sure some people will overindulge it, but if you have an intended purpose in mind, you will be safe.

Facebook for me was a new box in terms of motivating others. Many organizations and teams focus on people. The

Army is one of the biggest advocates of this philosophy. When your organization is about people, it is only natural to want the leaders of that organization to be in close contact and "up close and personal" with people.

In a fast-paced and changing world, old ideas sometimes need to be replaced with new ones or scrapped altogether. New and exciting technology has changed how we live our lives, young and old alike. Email, Facebook, Twitter, Linkedin, etc. have all changed how we communicate and share information. It is not uncommon for a "baby-boomer" to communicate with the "iGeneration" via Facebook; that is just the way it is these days.

I am a firm believer in face-to-face leadership, but sometimes old dogs have to learn new tricks. Networked socialization is something that is here to stay. Distributed motivation is simply an off-shoot of this phenomenon. No person can move faster than the electrons of an email, a "tweet," or Facebook post or reach the depth of an organization quicker than these means. This doesn't mean that face-to-face leadership needs to be thrown out the window; to me it simply means that you have to adapt and leverage the new technology at hand. As the saying goes, "If you can't beat them, join them."

As an example, I recently saw a note about a high-ranking military leader who banned social media in his command. No Facebook, tweeting, etc. I happen to know this leader and he is what many would call an "old school" leader. He is all about getting out, meeting people face-to-face. I am also 100 percent all about the old school way of business in terms of leadership. However, given my acceptance of how things are today, I could only wonder as I read this email, how much is this leader going to miss out on? It will be impossible to get out and see everything, hear everything and really keep a pulse on his unit. As a guess, he has just shut out at least 30 percent of information.

Social media doesn't have to cut against the grain of your personal values and beliefs. A simple rule is to figure out your purpose for using and engaging in social media activities. My purpose was to distribute motivation; plain and simple.

Networking via social media has allowed people to become comfortable with being impersonal. Therefore, as a leader, one must be prepared for both the good and bad of social media tools. It allows people to express themselves, but affords you to the opportunity connect with those you may otherwise have not noticed within your organization. Informality is the beauty of social media, but military leaders and/or executives at times become uncomfortable with informality. In order to retain control of what you want to achieve as a leader, keep a clear purpose in mind for your use of social media. However, you have to recognize that what you think should apply as rules for social media don't necessarily matchup with the greater society. Barring anything illegal, immoral, or unethical, if you can't handle the territory that comes with social media, then putting a ban on it for yourself may not be a bad idea.

As a leadership tool, social networking provides several advantages and disadvantages. Everyone can see and read what you post. There are ways to manipulate the settings to avoid this, but transparency is a good thing with regard to leadership.

Social media provides you with a high-speed way of communicating. Answering questions or disseminating information to a group takes less time than ever. In the Army we have a saying about emails, "message sent does not always mean message received." However, this rule didn't consider Android phones, iPhones, etc., or the network itself. I am still uncomfortable with the amount of people who are continuously in the neck-bent and two-thumb tango with their phones or Blackberries. People access information virtually 24 hours a day these days, not because they have to, but because they want to. With the thirst for information being so great these days, why not leverage it to your advantage?

The earlier mentioned advantages can easily become disadvantages; it all depends on your purpose for using social media as a leadership tool. The speed of disseminating information, the impersonal nature, and the 24 hour means of accessing information could backfire in an instant. As an example, if you use it as your primary means of distributing information, be sure that your information is accurate. "We have tomorrow off!" then an hour later, you have to recant your post... "Sorry, my bad, we have to work tomorrow." You begin to lose credibility quickly. This is okay for the followers, but not the leader. By no means am I suggesting that social media is a substitute for good leadership; it is an enabler of good leadership. You have to use it in a way that you feel will augment your leadership goals and philosophy.

My hope was to affect at least one person. If it affected two, great! If helped more, even better! Over time, I began to see others within the organization imitating this and it made me realize that distribution of motivational posts was catching on. Others were trying to motivate and inspire others. If your purpose is other than this, a social media context for leadership may not be right for you.

Many of us know that we all get tired of reading posts like "ugggghhhh... gotta go to class today." Sure you feel good about your post, but what did it do for anybody else? I wanted to do something for someone else. Facebook posts to me were an extension of one of the Army values that I have come to know and live; selfless service. What can I do or say to help someone else today? This is the question that guides my daily posts.

This may not appeal to you as a leader, but if you are going to use social media, make it count for those in your organization. Post something that makes others think or better yet, ask for suggestions. Social media should be a positive leadership tool. Do whatever you are comfortable with, be creative, take the good with the bad, but most of all try to use it as an extension of your leadership, not as a substitute.

If you are a leader at any level, it is well worth the time to invest a great deal of personal energy in people. No organization succeeds, or should I say succeeded, at a high level without a significant investment in people. If that investment is in the form of notes of encouragement, words of wisdom, or Facebook posts, it is time well spent. Think of the time when it would have been nice to hear those words, meet that person, or read that quote that would have taken you over the hump or made your outlook on something brighter.

> **Soldier Quote: Jonil Owimwrin,** "Sometimes you have to take the initiative and lead yourself or a group in the right direction because you know it's morally right. There are leaders and followers in life. It's much easier to walk down a paved road than it is to pave your own road for others to use behind you."

Chapter 8

DRIVE

Pebbles: Ask yourself this week . . . what drives me? Then ask, how hard are you driven? If it isn't 100 percent, seek another source. Whatever drives you (money, love, work, others, etc.) should drive you 100%. Get pumped up . . . do something!

The memory of an old Tiger Woods commercial inspired the above quote. Before you roll your eyes or sigh, this chapter is not about Tiger. One thing you can't deny about Tiger as a young golfer was his drive. The commercial that I remembered showed Tiger practicing in various weather conditions and at various times. At the end of the commercial, his question was simple, "Are you driven?" That simple statement always made me ask myself that very question from that day forward. Am I driven? And if so, what drives me? The one thing that allows a person to channel and focus their motivation is an objective. This, in essence, creates a drive. I define an objective in this case as being something other than a short-term goal.

You may not think of your short-term goals as connected to an overall objective. But, if you start to connect the dots, you will find that many short-term goals can lead you toward or away from your ultimate objective. Similar to a frog whose goal is to reach the other side of the pond; jumping from lily pad to lily pad is the short-term approach to achieving a bigger objective. How fast the frog obtains this objective depends on his approach. Sometimes people do not make these connections of short-term goals to larger objectives. They either spend time repeatedly jumping from one short-term goal to the next, unsure of where it will lead them, and expend a lot of energy in the process.

The frog has one objective: get to the other side of the pond. In a popular 80s Atari video game, *Frogger,* this was the sole objective; getting the frog to the other side without landing in the water. In order to sustain a high level of motivation, you must figure out what your objectives are. Moving from one short-term goal to the next gives you purpose, and that purpose gives you drive; now your drive serves to motivate you and vice versa. Otherwise, we move from one short-term goal to the next without feeling a sense of accomplishment. Given we have used a lot of energy and time in the process, we tend to become frustrated and this in turn affects our motivation.

We should never waste time or energy in achieving our objectives. Some people make the connections easily, and for others it seems to be unending frustration. The difference is that one person makes the connections and pursues the short-term goals in a path that leads directly to the objective. On the other hand, the frustrated person sees a lake full of lily pads, the other side of the pond, and what appears to be a daunting task of getting to the other side.

If you are one who can easily make connections of short-term goals and chart clear paths of one goal to the next, this is a gift that you can help others develop. I have met several individuals who either don't have goals, never put much thought into them, or never had anyone take the time to assist them in developing their goals. As a leader, your goal is to help others make connections and in some cases chart clear paths. This becomes your contribution to inspiring others.

It is amazing to watch a person who is totally driven. It is relatively easy to watch TV and spot a driven athlete like NBA player Kevin Durant or the NFL's Eli Manning. They stand head and shoulders above the rest. The scoring leader, the rebound leader, the undefeated heavyweight champion: can you imagine the time and effort they put into their profession to be the best? The amount of drive it takes to train, train, and then train some more? Some will say that they are driven by money, which may in part be true, but why doesn't every million dollar athlete perform at the same level? There is something else that drives the top performer. Think about Michael Jordan or Wayne Gretzsky; these athletes simply pounded the competition into submission. It wasn't good enough just to win. Their motivation was to simply be the greatest of all time while destroying the will of others to compete. It would be awesome to live in a world where everyone was that driven about all things. This may never be possible, but one thing is for sure: you can be just as driven.

Figure out what you want to achieve. What do you really want to be when you grow up? What in life do you desire to accomplish the most? Once you have settled on it, don't let anything stand in your way. This becomes your driving factor. Sure, you may not be able to chart a direct path to this goal, and this is probably where most lose their drive toward their objective. It simply becomes too hard to keep pressing forward, because in typical fashion, we want to arrive at that objective yesterday.

In most cases, we all have to set intermediate objectives along the way. You can't just plot a course to being a doctor or general officer in a couple of years. First there is college and everything that comes with it to include the financial burden, then there is time required where you will have to work your way through the ranks, and oh, don't forget to include a couple of setbacks in there at some point. Let's call these setbacks friction points or negative events. "Negative events and people teach us what we don't want so we can focus our energy on what we do want."[15] Your will and determination versus that of everybody and everything else allows you to deal with friction.

The vast majority of us have to weather the storm of frictions (big or small) to get where we want to go. The difference between you and the next person is who will stop pursuing their objective at the first sign of friction? Most of us want lives without friction, but when friction comes our way, so too should a will to overcome it every time. Whatever drives you has to drive you 100 percent. If it doesn't, you have not fully committed to achieving your objective.

The biggest friction you will encounter is other people! In some cases you will find more detractors than you will supporters. If you are moving past the crowd, someone in the crowd will want to pull you back simply because you are surpassing them. Have you ever heard comments like these before: "Why are you going to college?" "Why do you want to be a soldier, nurse, teacher, etc.?" "You are wasting your time pursuing that, you should focus on something else." Take these comments in one ear and quickly let them flow out the other. Add this to your fuel tank and keep pressing, or as I would commonly tell Soldiers, "Keep swinging." You will strike out on occasion, but never stop swinging; a home run is always a swing away. One of my favorite sayings: "Life is a test. Every adversity helps us grow."[16]

On that note, I absolutely must share this quick story. Early during my high school senior year, I went in to see the guidance counselor. I'll refer to her by a fictional name, Mrs. Smith. At any rate, Mrs. Smith was a nice enough person and well-liked by the vast majority of students in the school including myself. The conversation I had with Mrs. Smith struck a chord in my life that has driven me ever since.

I went into her office with the intent of inquiring about college opportunities and a request for her help to get me closer to this goal. As a guidance counselor, this is exactly what she was supposed to do, give guidance. The guidance that I received really shocked me. Mrs. Smith proceeded to tell me that I should pursue a vocational school or trade job. Granted, I had already taken steps (short-term goals) to help myself by enrolling in a few AP (Advance Placement) courses, but this had no bearing on her thought process. I was simply not college material in her view and it was her intent to convince me of that. I felt good that I was at least trying to help myself and the only thing I needed was "guidance" or a steer in the right direction. I received neither.

All I can say is that, given a successful military career, one undergraduate and two graduate degrees is *Thank you Mrs. Smith* for offering the fuel I needed to succeed and earn a college degree! Sometimes a little negative energy can also be turned into your driving factor. Mrs. Smith's words alone drove me 100 percent from that day forward and they still do.

The rules of the pond (in case you like the lily pad analogy), are to:

1. Determine where you want to go or where you want to be.
2. Chart a clear path, directly or indirectly, to your objective.
3. Factor in setbacks where you think you will encounter them (e.g. not completing a course on time, failure to get a certain job that you expected, a delay in a promotion, etc.).
4. Brace yourself mentally for the naysayers. ("Why are you pursuing that?")
5. Give 100 percent to every small goal that you establish.

These rules are not 100 percent guaranteed, but they are a start. All you need to know is where to start. Your drive will take you the rest of the way, but you must remain committed. There will always be friction along the way. When you stumble into those frictions, refer to rule No. 5.

Quote from a Soldier: Urbahn Rosas, "Drive is what makes all the difference. It makes civilians into soldiers, soldiers into warriors, and warriors into the leaders of tomorrow. It makes a person say yes I do wanna jump from an airplane; yes I do wanna wear a tan beret! [tan berets are worn by the U.S. Army's elite Ranger Regiment] Drive does indeed make all the difference."

Quote from a Soldier: Iveth N Brayan Sandoval, "The answer falls within the question, 'what do you want'? The majority of us go through life, often very successfully, without ever asking, much less answering, this most basic question. The most basic answer of course is that you want to express yourself fully, for that is the most basic human drive. We all want our voices to be heard and that has led some of us to the peaks and some of us to the depths."

Quote from a Soldier: Rob Rollins, "You have to have drive to be self-motivated in order to give motivation to your soldiers so that they become better people . . ."

Chapter 9

INVESTING

Pebbles: You only get out what you put in. If you are not achieving what you desire to achieve, you need to make a bigger deposit.

You only get what you put in. You have probably heard a similar saying or words to this effect. One funny way of looking at it in military jargon terms is "tiny heart syndrome"—a lack of heart and intestinal fortitude to achieve anything worth achieving. If you or others around you are suffering from "tiny heart syndrome" it will be tough to accomplish much of anything. The frustration that comes along with "tiny heart syndrome" is endless. The blame goes in every direction except the one in the mirror. Face it, this is the easiest course of action; blame someone else for your failures, your lack of achievement, or your inability to change whatever it is that you desire to change. If you aren't investing 100 percent of your mind and body to accomplishing your goals, you can pretty much call it quits on trying to achieve those goals. Half-hearted efforts and success do not go well together.

During my two-year tenure in 2nd Battalion, 9th Infantry Regiment, we participated in a 25-mile foot march with full combat gear to include what we term "rucksacks" (military backpack), every six months. This equated to four marches during a two-year tenure. This may not sound like a very arduous task, but try walking 25 miles with just regular, everyday gear. It is a little tougher than it may sound.

As a unit, the goal was always to remain in shape for many reasons other than this biannual event. More than 95 percent of those soldiers accomplished the march simply based on the level of unit physical fitness. This excludes those who were already injured, ill, and could not participate. There are three key factors that level the playing field for this event for any individual in the unit regardless of level of physical fitness: weather, terrain, and heart size (figuratively speaking).

Typically, one march occurred during summer and one during winter. In the Republic of Korea the winters are bitterly cold and the summers blistering hot, not including the high-humidity-index level. The terrain of Korea is extremely hilly. I assume that it ranks as one of the top hilliest places in the world. Inclines can range from a few meters to a few hundred meters in a direction that almost seems vertical. Unless you walk on the improved highways (which is never the case), a hilly 25-mile course is the end product every time. With an equipment load of 35-40 pounds not including water, the weight seems bearable for at least the first half of the course. Marches occurred at night, usually a late evening start after sunset with a completion at or just before sunrise. Due to the steep decline in nightly temperatures and the dangers of the hilly terrain, exceptions were made for the winter marches.

There are no iPods or iPhones allowed, no comfortable sneakers, or as we consider it, other "civilian" comfort items allowed. You have the companionship of many of your closest friends, and the solace of the open and hilly roads ahead of you. Any questions?

The conversations during the march consist of only those that are required or necessary. The posture for carrying weapons is as if you would encounter an enemy at any moment, a posture we commonly refer to as "ready." What this small detail implies is that all parts of your body are committed to every aspect of the 25 miles ahead. Your back is carrying the weight of your 35-40 pounds of gear and your head is supporting a helmet that weighs a couple of pounds. The same applies to your hands and arms that carry your assigned rifle weighing a few pounds. Your feet bear the entire load; and your mental focus is dedicated to not tripping or falling in the dark due to potholes, rocks, or other. There is however, a goal in mind and that is completing the march with your unit.

The individual award is a belt buckle only authorized to units in the Army that have an affiliation to the 9th Infantry Regiment. As of 2012, there were only two units that had the distinction of carrying this affiliation, 2-9 Infantry, in the Republic of South Korea and 4-9 Infantry, at Ft. Lewis Washington. The belt buckle was authorized by military act in 1925 as tribute to the heraldry of the regiment for actions in 1900 during the Boxer Rebellion. The soldiers of this period walked 85 miles into a fierce battle. The march conducted these days only replicates a portion of the original 85 miles. At the completion of the march, soldiers are awarded the "Manchu" buckle. The buckle is a metal replica of the unit symbol; a five-toed Chinese Imperial Dragon.

For many, it was a source of pride within the unit and a significant way to impress upon yourself and others that you were a contributor to the team. As I stated earlier, many with an above-average level of physical fitness would routinely not have an issue with completing the march, but inevitably would be sore the next morning. Even the soldier with an average level of fitness would not have a significant issue completing the march. The one thing that was for certain was that if you didn't commit 100 percent of your heart to completing the march, you would not finish.

The challenge of the environment alone could deter most from ever wanting to start the march. In some cases the temperatures were so cold that canteens would freeze if they were not placed inside of your rucksack. In the summer, the high level of humidity could make you feel as if you had gone swimming prior to the start of the march. Once you factor in the darkness and all that it brings along with it, your mind can sometimes do some funny things. If you had any shadow of a doubt about completing, chances are you were not going to succeed. The heat, cold, darkness, or heaviness of the load only served to hasten defeat if you were not totally committed to the goal of completion.

For four of these marches, I watched the unit complete this endeavor with an average completion rate of 95 percent. This is not bad at all considering the sheer size of the organization. There are three contributing factors to such a high success rate. The first is companionship. There was always someone around you to encourage you

The Rock

and keep you motivated. The second was the soldier's individual conditioning, and last but not least was the soldier's heart. I witnessed tremendous displays of heart during the course of the march. After the completion of the march, you could see the anguish on the faces of Soldiers from the bodily aches and pains. In some cases tears would roll down their cheeks as they received their buckle.

The first thing that was always identified as an issue that would test your heart even more than the other conditions that I previously outlined were your feet! Much could be done to take care of your feet, and given the years of experience available in all Army units, there are always tricks of the trade to be learned. Having problems with your feet during a march is similar to a sniper having a bad trigger finger; not a good sign. Nonetheless, there were always cases of soldiers who had prepared properly, equipped properly, but had something go wrong with their feet. As the saying would go for these marches, "once your feet go, you go." Your feet are your primary means of transportation for this event, so the saying was appropriate. Have you ever tried to drive with four flat tires? If that were to ever happen, you would probably go no farther than a few feet without risking damage to other parts of the car. The same logic applies to your feet under these circumstances, or so you would think, right? The answer is no.

The reward of receiving a belt buckle, being considered part of the team, or the fact that you didn't want to let your squad, platoon or yourself down usually overrode the aches, pains, and foot problems. There were many amazing stories of Soldiers completing this 25 miles with the equivalent of four flat tires. There are circumstances where it is mandatory to direct a Soldier to stop walking—signs of dehydration as an example. Nonetheless, in displays of heart, there are soldiers who will keep their pain hidden, motivation high, and inspiration fully intact in order to achieve their goal.

I attribute this to the level of heart that they display. The mental toughness displayed to complete the event despite a tremendous level of pain is commendable. For some, this was the hardest thing they will do short of combat operations, and for others it is a test of their own personal fortitude that they want to prove. Despite all the pain and challenges associated with it, there are many displays of heart that are guided by that individual's determination, level of self-motivation, and ability to mentally will their way to the finish.

In sports we give athletes huge credit for playing injured or hurt. The counter—argument is that these athletes are being paid millions of dollars to amaze and entertain. In the case of the foot marches, there are no million-dollar contracts, no championships, and no real entertainment value except the usual chuckle of someone poking fun at their buddy. So where does this level of determination come from? And why do I insist on referring to something that is seemingly intangible like "heart?" And what does it have to do with being motivated and inspired?

Things are never simple, but I like to think of them that way. It is true that heart really isn't measureable in the sense we generally think of it. One thing for sure is that when we refer to it, we all generally have the same level of understanding. It is a commonly used phrase . . . "That guy or gal really has heart." I could have used many other examples, even combat examples, but my goal was

The Rock

to show how this applies to a large organization over a short period of time. Every individual is separated by some degree of physical distance during this march, but then again, they are all connected at the same time. Everyone depends on everyone. Team leaders are depending on their team members, squad leaders depending on their squad members, and vice versa. It takes everyone to inspire and motivate others during an event of this nature. However, the one thing that you can't share is your heart.

When your motivation reserves start to run low, the pain kicks in, and when your drive is leaving you quicker by the step, the one thing that pulls it all back together is your heart. It may at times be a last-ditch effort, but it is your "failsafe mechanism;" kind of like a surge protector. It prevents all your other systems from being shorted out when there has been a significant drain on them. The drive to finish with your team may get you to the finish line, but it may wane over time. Even the encouraging words of others stop having appeal after about mile 19.

The one thing that gets all your main systems back "online", motivation, drive, dreams, etc. is your heart. It is the reserve that physically and literally gets you through the last few miles. In this case, the logic fits perfectly, but it applies to many other things as well. You see it all around you on a constant basis. Think about the worst situation you have been in and then think of the thing that could have mad that bad situation even worse. There are daily stories of events like this and people manage to come out of them better than before. Think of Hurricane Katrina victims; think of the 9/11 victims, etc. When you hear about these same victims pulling their lives back together and doing great and wonderful things, you wonder what gave them the will. Resilience is the standard answer and I agree, but I would argue that it was heart that allowed this resilience to shine through. This may be an over-simplification and some may see resiliency and heart as being synonymous. I could only imagine that in the worst of moments, everything abandoned them, motivation, drive, you name it. Something had to provide the spark to get their other internal systems back on line one by one. Call it necessity, call it determination, or whatever you desire, but I prefer to refer to it as heart.

No one ever achieved much with "halfhearted" effort. It takes absolute dedication and synchronization of all the "internal systems" that you have in order to achieve the desired goal. It is acceptable to change your objective if desired, but do not change it simply because you have given up, or lost the desire to put forth the level of energy required.

When things are at a low point and desperation is the only thing you have left, you must spend your last bit of reserves. There is no use in saving your emotional reserves for a later date. Saving it for a rainy day or the next objective will not help your cause for today. Unlike saving money, you must use your emotional reserves when you need them most. They certainly do not accumulate interest over time. If you do not expend your emotional reserve when you need it most, you will continue to procrastinate and eventually look back and say, "I wish I would have." It is somewhat faulty logic to apply the thought process that you will give a half effort to achieve one objective and full effort to achieve another. Chances are you will end up committing a half effort to both.

Anything worth achieving takes effort. There is often pain associated with that effort and there are things that can't make that pain disappear; pep talks, wishful thinking, or inaction. You have to dig deep in order to go the extra mile, that is your heart in action.

Quote from a Relative: Edna Calwise-Starks, "Your best is always enough, no matter how small."

Verse given by a Relative: Susie Gray, "And do not be conformed to this world, but be transformed by the renewing of your mind, that you may prove what the will of God is, that which is good and acceptable and perfect." Romans 12:2

Chapter 10

DREAM BIG

Pebbles: Never stop dreaming . . . if you give up your desire to dream, you have given up; dreams without action are just that—dreams. Act on your dreams . . . and dream BIG!

The next time you are having a discussion with one of your subordinates or peers, ask him or her about dreams. This may seem like a pretty personal and invasive question to ask, but it's one that is very insightful. If there is a pause longer than several seconds . . . say 30 seconds, it probably indicates that the individual hasn't given much thought to their dreams and aspirations. I found that very few of the junior Soldiers who I encountered had actually given thought to their future or their dreams. This was a bit disturbing. Many were not encouraged to dream.

When individuals are encouraged to articulate and fulfill their dreams and have a support network to help them; the benefits are tremendous. Individual confidence increases, motivation may increase, and a happier, more confident individual emerges within the organization.

If people are not confident or motivated enough to pursue their dreams, it is up to the leader to encourage and reinforce that dreams are attainable. In some cases, individuals only need a push in the right direction to set them on the path for success. A letter of recommendation is one powerful tool a leader can use to help this process.

For example, in some cases I found that soldiers rarely think about their dreams of obtaining a college degree. Becoming an officer or warrant officer, attending college, or even seeking selection for special operations is the aspirations of many Soldiers. But only a few would share these goals if they felt they could receive genuine support in pursuing those dreams. If I learned this was something an individual aspired to do, I would try to determine how committed they were to the goal. This would reveal a wide spectrum of insights ranging from very little commitment to significant commitment. Regardless, I would try to figure out my role in fostering this individual's drive toward the pursuit of this dream; in most cases it would be through a letter of recommendation. For the military leader, this again, is not a novel concept in and of itself. What I did find interesting was that the speed at which I could follow up with these letters was the real key to success. If you as a leader are viewed as being more aggressive than the individual about helping him achieve his dream, chances are, he will be ignited by your level of enthusiasm. If a Soldier needed a letter of recommendation, my standard was 24-48 hours for a return product. Once delivered, the ball was clearly in their court. This now allowed me to continue my encouragement, especially if I was starting with an individual who hadn't invested a lot of commitment in his own goals. It now allowed me to ask the question, "Where are you with completing your packet?" "Or how is the process going to get admitted into X?" This approach is not designed as a guilt trip, but as a way for the leader to seize the initiative. The desired outcome is to have the individual wrestle the initiative back from you, take charge of the process. The hope is that the boost you provided was enough to inspire him to see his dream through to reality. People need encouragement to achieve their dreams. Remember my experience with Mrs. Smith?

As a leader, you must encourage your subordinates to dream and dream big. It may take days, weeks, or even months of encouragement for an individual to muster enough courage to pursue a dream that she may have initially thought unattainable. You as a leader can facilitate and may even expedite that process. Your confidence in their ability to "dream big and achieve big" is one more way to motivate anyone in any organization.

Your efforts on their behalf are especially important for your young Soldiers or employees. For example, you could introduce a young person to someone who successfully pursued and obtained the same dream. Nothing is better than a real-world example. Every path will not be the same for all individuals, but somebody has walked a similar path in most cases. Knowing where the stumbling blocks are along the way is half the work. In this case, they have just been given another "source" of inspiration that we discussed in previous chapters. "If he did it, so can I!" This is exactly the attitude that you want to instill.

When others share their stories of success, they sometimes make the error of only sharing the easy aspects

The Rock

of the accomplishment. It is always simple to say how easy something was once we have accomplished it. Conversely, over-exaggerating how difficult achieving a goal is a common pitfall as well. Young Soldiers often ask about various types of qualification courses such as Airborne, Air Assault, Ranger School, etc. Some leaders take the approach of impressing how hard it was when they did it and the associated horror stories of accomplishing the endeavor. Be leery of adding to the legacy of how hard it was when you achieved a certain goal. Keep in mind who you are talking to when it comes to the pursuit of dreams. You can easily inspire and just as quickly "un-inspire" simply based on your approach. You must find a balance: be candid enough to share your perspective of achieving something without over-emphasizing how easy or difficult it was to accomplish a certain goal.

In the military, experienced leaders are good judges of those who can or cannot attend certain courses based on an evaluation of an individual's skills, competency, readiness, etc. Nonetheless, leader encouragement plays a role in enabling subordinates to successfully achieve a goal. Experience comes into play when one has to be honest with a subordinate. There is a fine line between honesty and disparaging words. More importantly, you want the individual to come to grips with an honest assessment of his or her abilities, skills, competency, etc. On the other hand, you don't want an honest assessment interpreted as criticism. It takes a little skill to guide an individual to the realization that you are being constructive versus destructive. You don't want the individual to walk away from the conversation only to view you as a fault-finder.

My grandmother was a master of guiding me to realizations of my own faults in a constructive and caring way. Her simple saying "your eyes are bigger than your stomach," helped put a lot of things into perspective. Initially, I never quite understood what she meant by this saying. My grandmother was a tremendous cook and whenever it was time to eat, I would pile my plate as high as possible with all the great things she had prepared. She would say, "your eyes are bigger than your stomach," and based on her experience and wisdom, she knew that I wouldn't eat it all. I, on the other hand, begged to differ. I didn't know what she knew and couldn't see what she saw. She wasn't fault finding, but rather merely stating a fact that I myself couldn't see. My eyes were bigger than my stomach and I didn't eat all that I had placed on my plate. My eyes and stomach were not in good communication with each other.

Individuals who pursue their dreams may also have some disconnect between their desires (eyes) and drive (stomach) to reach a certain goal. Good leaders have the same ability to point out this disconnect without being discouraging. Sometimes individuals dream big and have the right intentions, but simply aren't ready for the task at hand. They feel that they are, but you as a leader know better. Don't discourage the individual and if you happen to be this individual, be honest with yourself first and foremost. Be able to recognize constructive criticism from fault finding.

Good leaders constructively criticize and poor leaders find fault. The difference being constructive criticism comes with solutions and fault finding does not. The good leader will find a way to help you get to where you want to be. In the case of my grandmother and I, she would make me return food and start with smaller size servings. Once my ego settled, I realized that she was right. Good

The Rock

leaders point out that you can't eat the entire elephant in one bite, and are willing to recommend ways to get there. This is how you distinguish constructive criticism from fault finding.

As an example of this, I had a young lieutenant who desperately wanted to apply for and attend U.S. Army Ranger School, Fort Benning, Georgia. Ranger school is a grueling 61-day combat leadership course that focuses on small-unit tactics in austere and extreme conditions. It has been called the "toughest combat course in the world."[17] As the approving authority for endorsing his request, I knew that he wasn't prepared or ready for the course; deep down, I think he realized this as well. For the better part of a year, we would talk and our conversations always sounded like this:

Lieutenant: "Sir, I'm ready to go to Ranger school."
Me: "Where is your packet?"
Lieutenant: "I'm still working on it."

Throughout this process, I never discouraged him and always stood willing and ready to approve his packet (series of prerequisites) once he demonstrated that he was ready. Having attended the course myself, I offered plenty of advice, and I know from observation that he acted on much of it, but not all of it. He still had a rough time admitting to himself that he wasn't quite ready. His eyes in this case were clearly bigger than his stomach.

I give him credit for being persistent, but not patient. After departing the unit, the lieutenant contacted me a year later, only this time to say that he had undoubtedly faced his shortfalls and gotten himself prepared to attend the course. But there was a problem; his new boss was not at all supportive. When the lieutenant approached his new boss, he was given little encouragement, and sent on his merry way. Sure, there may be other points to the story that could have weighed in on this interaction, but the idea here is that interactions of this nature crush dreams in an instant. On a personal level you have to determine if this will deter you or increase your resolve to obtain the dream. On a professional level, you will have to re-chart a new course to the objective. Remaining committed to your dreams is essential. It has taken me years in some cases to attend courses that I desired or needed in my military career, but in all cases, small detours along the way didn't prevent me from getting there.

As a leader, recognize your role in the process of encouraging others. Use your knowledge to help rather than to hinder. More importantly, if you don't honestly see someone achieving a goal because her "eyes are too big," let her know why. Point out that you are not finding fault, and provide some recommendations to help get her to where she wants to be. In some cases you may have to refer her to someone with greater expertise than you. At least you are facilitating and not impeding someone from pursuing her dreams.

> **Quote from a Soldier:** *Alex Braden,* "Dreams are the sparks that call us do something more or go farther than we have before. When we have the determination to make them reality; dreams become goals. How do we commit to them? We think through the process to make the daunting increasingly more possible, and any foreseen risks worth the cost."

Quote from a Soldier: Erik Choquette on committing to dreams and goals, "Easy, I keep my head low and my ruck high." [ruck is a common reference to a military style backpack]

Quote from a Soldier: Larry Sack, "Dream is an image you are trying to draw in your mind but Goals are when an individual comes to full understanding of that dream. Most fill fulfill them because they try to commit in the drawing phase."

Chapter 11

FUN

Pebbles: We were all more fun as kids because we had the natural ability to laugh at ourselves; somewhere that got lost for some of us. Try to find it and you as well as others will enjoy being around you!

When people think of motivation, it is generally associated with positive images: joy, excitement, or determination. This is the positive connotation associated with motivation that generally comes to mind. For every source of external motivation, there are an equal number of internal things to keep people inspired. I will not try to capture all of these things, but I would like to focus on one—fun.

Besides, what is being motivated if it is not fun? In case you are not yet convinced about the whole positive or negative motivation thing, try this exercise on for size. Think of the chore that you most dislike (cutting grass, washing dishes, etc.). We routinely get things like this done because we are motivated to just "git r dun." We are inspired by the fact that once complete, our yard will be the best looking on the block, or dishes won't be waiting in the sink in the morning. The point is, we may not be happy or overjoyed by the task, but we are, to a lesser extent, motivated to get it done. If this exercise didn't win the argument, I will make another attempt at it later.

The point is, motivation may not always be positive in nature, depending on what the purpose is behind achieving a goal. This is where the "kids" model comes in handy. Kids are generally determined to make anything they do fun. Even if it is a task that is not preferred, they become easily distracted by the one thing that will bring the joy back to their lives. To make things fair, I will define kids as those 2-11 years old. Whether you give them the task to sit quietly in the corner or pickup their toys, they will find a way to entertain themselves and make it fun. This usually takes the form of not sitting quietly for very long or the task of picking up toys quickly turns into playing with the toys. Kids also find it easy to find laughter in a majority of the things they do. Just one trip to a day care center and you will see my point; there are not a lot of unhappy faces there. Kids may not invest a great deal of time in thinking about what they do. But a majority of the time, having fun is a No. 1 priority.

In *Drive*, author Daniel H. Pink describes this phenomenon of fun in a slightly different way. Pink describes the term "autotelic experiences," a term developed by Mihaly Csikszentmihalti, a leading American psychologist.[18] Autotelic is derived from the Greek auto (self) and telos (goal or purpose).[19] In developing this term, Csikszentmihalti did research on children playing. His goal was to explore the "positive, innovative, and creative approaches to life."[20] What he discovered is that child's play was self-fulfilling and that the act itself was the reward.

Csikszentmihalti later changed the term autotelic to "flow."[21] Flow was used to describe optimal moments in people's lives or satisfying experiences. Pink states that "when a person is in *flow*, goals are clear; you have to reach the top of the mountain; you have to hit the ball across the net, etc."[22] In other words, when a person is in flow he enjoys doing what he does and sees the goal as achievable. Throughout Csikszentmihalti's research, the basic foundation is the reference to child's play.

However, Csikszentmihalti realized that "flow" changes for many adults later in life. He describes this effect as follows:

> "Children careen from one flow moment to another, animated by a sense of joy, equipped with a mindset of possibility, and working with the dedication of a West Point cadet. Then—at some point in their lives—they don't. What happens? Csikszentmihalti explains, "You start to get ashamed that what you're doing is childish."[23]

As you pursue your goals and go through day-to-day activities, it is easy to lose sight of where the fun is in all of it. As Csikszentmihalti explains, you probably dismiss finding fun in what you are doing as childish. For the most part, we will look at the task at hand as not being fun. I have heard and read many great sayings in my career, but one of the best that I can remember is the saying that required you to ask yourself about the things you "get" to do versus the things you "have" to do.

The thought behind this saying is that, on many occasions, we lose the joy in what we are doing because in our eyes it becomes a burden and is not enjoyable. There are others out there who would love to have the opportunities that you have and would enjoy every minute of it. Think about the severely ill patient who would love to jog a few miles or take a walk in the park. The disabled child who would love to have the opportunity to play on his or her school's sports team. If we apply these examples to ourselves and our daily endeavors, we would hopefully retain the joy in whatever it is we are doing. Instead of waking and saying, "I *have* to go to work today," or "I *have* to go to class," reverse the thought and saying to, "I *get* to go to work today," or "I *get* to go to class today." The point is to change the phrase from a negative to a positive meaning. The goal is to reconnect with the "fun factor" associated with what you are doing. This will be difficult to apply to everything, but applying it during those days or times when things don't appear to be fun anymore is important.

Point one of having fun is to change your perspective. More specifically, changing your phrases from "have to" to "get to" goes a long way toward your personal motivation. Point two is to focus your perspective on yourself. Don't be quick to point blame elsewhere as a starting point. Sometimes looking at yourself first, allows you to find the brighter side of things. Laughing at yourself helps you realize that *you* took the fun out of what you are doing, not everyone around you. As the saying goes, "never take yourself too seriously."

I absolutely love the game of golf, but my problem is that I absolutely suck at it. Golf is supposed to be a fun sport. However, I have always had a difficult time having fun when most of my golf balls find their way into the woods, water, and sand; but never the green. This is compounded when you play with individuals who play the game very well. Their shots generally go where they would like and putts usually drop in less than two strokes. Additionally, this is accompanied by some level of trash talking that serves to further distract you. It makes you feel even worse and definitely takes the fun out of it. As a young captain, I learned a valuable lesson from one of my former non-commissioned officers, while playing the game of golf. It was not his words, but his actions that inspired me to want to continue playing the game. What did he do? He simply laughed at himself the entire time we played golf. He would routinely hit golf balls into the woods or water, and his reaction would be sheer laughter. He laughed at himself so hard at times, that he would make you break out into hysterical laughter along with him. He would make comments like "man I suck!" but what I observed each time we played was that he had fun and by default, so did I. He simply had something that I didn't have and that was the power to truly laugh at and with myself. It was an amazing thing to witness. Being able to laugh at ourselves is a great gift to have.

In the military it is sometimes hard to find those moments of finding fun in things, especially when our country is at war and there is much blood and treasure being lost on a daily basis. Due its nature, our profession requires a lot of things, but fun does not automatically come to mind as No. 1 on the list. There is not much fun in being shot at by an enemy or hit by an improvised explosive device (IED) while traveling from point A to point B. There is no fun to be had regarding this aspect of our military duties. The same could be said to be true about any profession or aspect of our lives. There are many reasons to take your profession, your family, and other important matters seriously, but finding fun within yourself and things that you do is essential to motivation. If you can't have fun with yourself, no one else will either. Like the kid who turns a not-so-fun task into fun, try to find that kid in you and make the not so fun—fun.

The sergeant I mentioned earlier would inspire me every time we played golf and I couldn't help but enjoy the day. You can infect others around you in the same way, but you must first start with the ability to laugh at yourself.

In the book *Emotional Intelligence* by Daniel Goleman, he stresses the importance of self-awareness, but he places an emphasis on having the ability to laugh at one's self:

> "People with strong self-awareness are realistic—neither overly self-critical nor naively hopeful. They are honest with themselves about themselves. They are honest about themselves with others, even to the point of being able to laugh at their own foibles."[24]

Leading others to laugh at you sometimes turns into getting them to laugh with you. Leaders especially tend not to want others to laugh at them, but you have to step above that level of personal pride. Showing the example that you can laugh at yourself will teach others the same. This is not intended to give approval to laugh off mistakes or anything serious in nature. It simply implies that 8 out of 10 times, there is probably some humor and fun to be found in the things that you do. Besides, this is a personal investment in you. There are more than enough people who are waiting to take your fun from you and the sad part is that you cannot change them one bit. However, you have all the power in the world to change yourself, so enjoy the person who knows how to laugh at himself. This is called "levity!" Enjoy your newfound levity!

> **Quote from a Soldier: Ken Nagata,** "There are two types of fun: 'Disneyland fun', which is when we allow our mind and bodies time to relax, and then there's 'building-your-house fun', which is when we use our time to improve ourselves. The most fun is when the activity contains both types."

Chapter 12

ME TIME

Pebbles: People who give a lot to others really deserve a little "me" time once in a while. Sometime this week, find some time to dedicate just to you (one minute or two hours, it doesn't matter), but take that time for yourself.

"You need to take some time off," or "You need to do something for yourself sometime." Have words like this ever been directed at you? When you think about it, your personal time is the most prized possession you have. I am assuming that time ranks at least in the top three things that are of importance to you. When and how do you make time for yourself if you are committed to dedicating a lot of time to others?

Thus far, I have dedicated a great deal of attention to helping leaders focus on others. As difficult as it may sound to carve out some free time of any day as "me" time is necessary. Taking the time to evaluate your own level motivation, contemplate goals, or just refresh your thoughts is necessary to retain your sanity and sense of balance.

Sometimes commitment to others prevents you from setting aside time for yourself. When selfless service is a top priority in your organization, finding time to dedicate to self may be difficult. As an example, in the Army we have a saying of "Mission First and People Always." Any military spouse who has been around longer than a day probably would tell you that this is one term they would prefer not to hear. It is the people that make, not only a military organization, but any organization. The Army takes this seriously as an organization, and some leaders understand it better than others. If a soldier is in need, or in trouble for that matter, it will require his leader's assistance. It is the leader's duty to be there for that individual. On the same note, if you are at a family outing and receive the call that Private Snoopy is involved in an incident and is in need of assistance, the leader in charge of that soldier will immediately make his or her way to that soldier to provide the needed assistance. This is the definition of selfless service. The family outing will have to wait until you return, or be continued later. This is why any military spouse is not so excited to hear that particular quote, but many of them understand and encourage this in support of soldiers and their spouses. They understand it, but it places a dilemma in the face of the leader. It is a continual process of "taking care of soldiers," doing whatever, being wherever, and accomplishing whatever is required for the benefit of the soldier and/or his or her family. If you are a leader without a significant other and depending on the level of need of your subordinates, you will still find it hard to carve out time for yourself.

The Rock

Regardless of the obstacles or challenges, the key to sustaining your personal motivation as a leader is to dedicate time for yourself. What I am referring to is the time to think and reflect. I am not referring to the time that you set aside for the gym or to participate in your favorite pastime, but there are those who would argue that this time counts as well. In his thoughts on reflection or what I call "me time", John Robbins, the son and nephew of the founders of Baskin-Robbins Ice Cream shops, described reflection as follows:

> "Some people do yoga and meditate, other people go run out in the woods, or dance, or pray, or keep a journal. There are so many ways. And it can be one thing for a few years and another thing for another few years; it can change form. The form isn't the point. Individuals have to find what works for them, but some way where you're answerable, not to society and not to making a living and not to other people's needs, but just to what's alive in you."[25]

Taking time for yourself could take you several minutes or several hours. I once heard a leader comment that leaders should find the time in their day every day to kick their feet up on the desk and simply think. At the time, I didn't really feel like this was a very profound statement. Based on everything that you may be responsible for and the things that consume your time throughout any given day, the time you find to kick your feet up is when you are kicking them up to get in the bed for a short night's sleep! The time that I am referring to is solely dedicated by you to you.

During your "me time," you must take time to reflect on a full spectrum things-certainly not all at once-such as what motivates you, your goals, problems, etc. This is your time to take a personal inventory of yourself. Are you aware of yourself? Are you in control of your emotions? Are you part of the problem, or is everyone else the problem? Are needed priorities still in the order to accomplish the objectives that you previously established? These are some of the reflections you may need to have as part of your personal inventory.

You may take this time to simply reflect on the events of the day up to that point, or you may prefer to think about things of tomorrow. The one thing that is important is to simply take the time for yourself and your personal sanity out of respect for your own level of motivation.

The other important aspect of reflecting during your "me time" is to think ahead. I recently read an article regarding retirement. The article revealed survey data that only a small percentage of the United States population properly save for retirement. Why? The results revealed that many people simply do not think that far ahead. They cannot bring their minds to grips with seeing themselves at 65 or older. When you think about it, ask yourself this same question. When was the last time you really saw yourself as a 65 year old doing whatever 65 year olds do? Like me, this is probably too much to get your arms around at the present moment, I am sure. You have to take the time to think and reflect on a lot of things. Thinking ahead is important because it allows you step away from the present and realize disconnects in your current activities that may take away from achieving future goals. The more often you dedicate time to reflecting, the less time it will take to do it.

Focus on one thing, one aspect of something, and go from there. Try not to overwhelm yourself in multiple problems or issues. You will be amazed at some of the thoughts that may cross your mind during this period of "me time." The beauty of it is that you can even pre-plan on things to think about. "Today, I am going to dedicate my 'me' time to reflecting on or thinking about (fill in the blank). Ask yourself hard questions about your level of motivation to do what you are currently doing or your commitment to continue doing what you are doing. Are you exhibiting "FEBA" (False Enthusiasm BS Attitude), or are you genuinely inspired and driven? These are questions only you can answer during this time, but the important thing is to take the time. No one will do this for you. You may even dedicate a great deal of time helping others see this, but once you have mastered it for yourself, share the wealth with others.

> **Quote from a Soldier: Jason Anderson,** "Everyone needs time to center themselves . . . to sit in careful reflection and take in everything that's happening."

> **Quote from a Soldier: Brian Manion,** "Me time is always important to gain perspective and reevaluate your priorities. And I don't know where it fits in, but it's a motto of mine, 'It doesn't matter how many times you get knocked down as long as you keep getting up.'"

Milford H. Beagle Jr.

Quote from a Soldier: Robert Vandervoort, Jr., "It is the time I need to myself to absorb all that is sent my way, and filter out garbage that I don't need to get through my day, week, month, year, and life."

Chapter 13

HUMILITY

Pebbles : Humility is a trait not often practiced by the masses. When you find your head in the clouds and your horse is a little higher than everyone else's, stop at the nearest bakery and order a piece of humble pie!

Humility has always been one of my favorite topics, or actually my favorite thing to observe in people. As my thought process outlines in this particular pebble, I feel that this is a trait seldom practiced by the masses. Have you ever encountered that person who has a lot to say and much boasting to do when things are going well? Now if by chance things are not going so well, this same person rarely has a few words to say about anything, with the exception of how screwed up things are considering they have now run into friction. What about the person who thanks only himself for being where he is? It would appear that no one helped them along the way. It was all their doing and not a single hand reached out at any point to pull them up a level. I love to observe and listen to these individuals. I truly get a kick out of their stories and their greatness. In some cases you would think that you were having a conversation with the world's greatest boxer Muhammad Ali: The Greatest of All Time (GOAT). Listening to them really makes me just crack up inside. Why?

To an extent these people really do see everything as being about them and without them the earth wouldn't rotate on its proper axis. It is really hilarious to listen to these individuals because it is simply amazing to believe that this person really buys so much of his/her own hype. This is also reflected in retired Gen. Colin Powell's *Leadership Secrets*; "Don't become so attached to your position that when your position goes, your ego goes with it."[26]

To illustrate the value the U.S. Army places on leadership positions; leaders in the Army are referred to as "green-tabbers." Green tabs are worn on formal and other authorized uniforms displayed under rank insignia to indicate that you are in a leadership position. Everyone recognizes you as being in a position where making tough decisions is a matter of routine, and your influence spans several levels. You have the ability to affect or influence many things: people, ideas, superiors, and subordinates alike. Your level of influence is unrivaled by your peers who may not be in those positions. This is regardless of the level of leadership position in which you serve.

To this end, there is a certain level of authority and responsibility that accompanies leadership positions. In some cases individuals will leave these positions and still attempt to exert authority that they are no longer authorized. Egos swell to the size of hot air balloons and you can absolutely forget making this person a follower ever again. As Gen. Powell alludes to, if your overblown ego is so closely linked to your position and the position goes, you are left reveling in a lot of your own hype and hopefully haven't created too many enemies in the process. The people who were stepped on and the bridges that you burned will eventually have to be repaired, and if you did a lot of damage based on the marriage of your ego and that position, you will have a lot of repair work to do. If you have to cross paths with one of those who you and your ego crossed, hope and pray that they are of a forgiving nature.

Another way of looking at a lack of humility or having an overblown ego is what I like to refer to as being "special." We are all special in our own way, special to a certain person, special to a certain group, etc. We all deserve to feel good about things we have accomplished and maybe even the things we have, but this does not give us the liberty to rub someone's nose in it.

If you are always focused on "you," it is really going to be difficult for you to focus on the team. As you become more complacent and feeling "special," there is someone just waiting to surpass you. The children's story about the "Tortoise and the Hare" illuminates this fact very well.

Think about the person you may have come in contact with who was not very humble; I would venture to say that you probably didn't get in too many words edge wise right? More than likely, it was all about them. Don't be that guy!

There are many people who look up to you as a leader. Without your realizing it, there may also be others who may look up to you also (children, relatives, friends, etc.). However, how you view others and how you view yourself in relation to others is really what matters the most. Being considerate to those that others may look down upon is a character trait worth developing. As a teenager, I learned many valuable lessons from my dad. One of the most memorable was his lesson on humility.

In my small home town of Enoree, S.C., we had this tree that was called the "Whino tree." I must pause to explain what a "whino tree" is; it was simply a congregating spot for the town's "elder statesmen." It was also a place to enjoy an alcoholic drink while enjoying the shade of a large pecan tree. The entertainment value of watching these men tell stories, get drunk, and tell more tall tales would have been worth the price of admission. As we drove by the tree one Saturday, my dad pointed out that I should never look down on another man, regardless of what his status in life appears to be. He pointed out several individuals under the tree and proceeded to tell their stories. To the untrained eye, many appeared to be run-of-the-mill drinkers who had nothing better to do than laugh, talk, or drown their sorrows in the drink of the day. But what he pointed out was a tree full of knowledge and skills.

He would point out one gentleman and tell me how he was a trained automotive mechanic and could fix anything with four wheels. He pointed out another and told me how he was a trained carpenter and could build any type of structure that your heart desired.

His bottom-line was this: "never make a snap impression on someone based on looks, or look down on someone because of what you assume." The other part of this lesson was that many of these individuals would go completely out of their way to help you. As fate would have it, I needed a minor car repair one day and I didn't have funds to take it to the automotive shop. So what did I do?

Drove to the tree, got a free repair, and the only payment I had to give in return was a simple "thank you sir."

Now my dad wasn't trying to impress upon me to stop at every "whino-tree" I encountered and congregate with the local drinkers; hopefully this point is obvious. So what does this have to do with humility, you may ask. Simple, don't attempt to be above the team or better than the team. You want to make the team, and those around you, better. Don't allow your position or ego to stand between you and a better organization for all involved. Contribute what you have versus talking about what you have. Be proud of what you have accomplished and who you have become, but don't allow it to consume you. If you were to lose the job, rank, or title, who would you be then? Think about it.

The link between humility and interpersonal skills is a more subtle relationship of my previous example but worthy of expanding upon. Leaders must have good interpersonal skills and an ability to deal with all people in order to have an effective organization. The Center of Creative Leadership found that executives who had low people-relating skills often failed. These executives expressed flaws such as being overly reactive, impatient, unable to delegate, engage, or motivate.[27]

In research conducted by Michael Lombardo and Cynthia McCauley, they use four areas to outline interpersonal problems that were linked to managerial failure:

1. Over ambition—alienating others on the way up, or worrying more about getting a promotion than about doing the current job

2. Independence—being a know-it-all or isolating oneself from others
3. Abrasiveness—bullying, insensitivity, or lack of caring
4. Lack of composure—being volatile and unpredictable toward others, often under pressure.[28]

Humility will take you very far with those around you. Conversely, you will encounter many problems if an overblown ego prevents you from connecting with people in your organization. A humble leader will not only work in your favor to gain cooperation from others, but will certainly inspire others to be themselves around you and not feel embarrassed because of their perceived inferiority. Demonstrating your desire to get others to your level or helping them get to a new level will increase motivation. As a leader, you must have the ability to check your ego at the door for the good of not only yourself, but others.

> **Quote from a Soldier: David Owen,** "Humility is that bit of leadership, and being a human being, that makes one better at both."
>
> **Quote from a Soldier: Erik Choquette,** "A leader who takes blame and passes credit."
>
> **Quote from a Soldier: Christian Stallings,** "Humility leads to strength and not to defeat. The greatest form of self-worth is to admit your shortcomings and to make amends for them. You must overcome all obstacles that are put in your path."

Chapter 14

LISTEN

Pebbles: Take time today to listen. For some this is a hard thing to do, but we were given two ears and one mouth for a reason. Listening helps you to understand, so if someone else's voice is more pleasing to your ears than your own . . . you have this figured out.

I have come to learn during life and during my time in the military that there are listeners and then there are talkers. Talkers do not want to hear anything anyone else has to say and seldom put their mouths on pause to receive anything others are saying.

In Army terms, we also have an expression for this, "transmitters and receivers." This is analogous to our communication devices, which are similar to those of police forces, and firemen. What is unique about these devices is that two people cannot talk at the same time, as they can on the phone. Trust me, this is a good thing. You must allow the other person to complete his transmission before you are allowed to transmit. To ensure that you are finished with your transmission, you must use the word "over." This lets the receiver know that you are finished with your transmission. A simple transmission would sound like: "Blue 6 this is Red 6, what is your location? Over!" "Red 6 this is Blue 6, I am at the north intersection. Over!" At any rate, you are either transmitting or receiving, but never both. How many times have you observed two people talking at each other because they are both talking at the same time? In this case, you can't tell who is talking and who is receiving.

This is probably one of the most important keys to motivating individuals within an organization. It can lead to lasting inspiration. There are a significant number of people within any level organization who want to be heard. As a leader, lending an ear to individuals at any level goes along way for the good of the organization. Trust me there are individuals who will have enough to say for the entire organization, so there will never be a shortage of finding those who have something to say. Finding those who do not have much to say or are bashful about speaking up is a much harder task. Building confidence sometimes comes as easy as just listening to those voices that rarely have much to say. If they won't come to you, you must go to them.

In some leadership circles, this is referred to as empowering individuals in the organization. Empowerment is the concept of a leader willing to involve others and solicit participation based on subordinates' knowledge and skills. Leaders who "empower others are good listeners and rely on collaboration rather than authoritative leadership."[29] To take this a step further, "they [leaders] are not compelled to do all the talking and

The Rock

resist imposing a solution on others unless the situation warrants."[30]

As a leader, it goes without saying that for you to ask the opinion of a subordinate or solicit their feedback on something minor may mean a lot to that person. In addition, if you act on a recommendation that a subordinate provides, look out; you may have just opened many new possibilities. Word will spread like wildfire that the boss actually listens! To some, listening goes beyond just opening your ears and absorbing information, it is about what you do with the information that was offered that matters most.

Another key dimension of listening, especially if it regards a superior to a subordinate, is the approach to listening. More times than not, the superior takes the lead in a conversation and instantly isolates the subordinate. This is not an open conversation, but a disguise for a conversation. What in effect will happen is that the subordinate begins to shut down versus open up. Why? Because they are solicited for input, but no output is received from the leader. There is a lot of take and very little give, and this in some cases will make a person begin to feel guarded as if there is nothing in it for them. The end result is a conversation that dries up shortly after the leader runs out of probing questions.

In most cases, the superior may have to break the ice in a conversation with a subordinate. However, some leaders may lack the skills to keep the conversation going without it appearing to be an interrogation session. The mark of a good conversation is one that allows the leader to listen and not feel the burden of trying to keep the conversation afloat. There may be many reasons behind this, but the one I most commonly encountered from subordinate leaders with regard to their subordinates was the claim of a lack of commonality. The general claim would sound like: "I don't have anything in common with any of my subordinates." The simple and short answer to this problem is to gain some commonalities!

True it is hard to gain commonalities with every single person, but it is the effort that counts. The leader has to always be above the fray in order to make a connection with subordinates. The simplest way to do this is to be inquisitive to those individuals you feel you may not have a connection with. It will not only generate conversation, but provide you with a learning opportunity that requires nothing more than your ability to listen.

Once I overheard one junior officer talking to another about problem soldiers in his platoon. During this conversation, the officer was complaining about a few individuals in his platoon who always seemed to have problems. He was very quick to point out that he simply didn't have the time to listen to or deal with all of these problems. The fact that he didn't want to invest the time to listen to these soldier's problems led me to believe that he was creating more problems. I expressed this to the young officer so that he could understand that preventing one small problem now prevents dealing with a larger problem later.

The young leader was doing his part in helping solve the problems, but he didn't realize that for the most part, he was addressing the symptoms and not the cure in a majority of the so-called problem cases. There are many instances where a leader can resolve a problem simply through the art of listening. Trying to solve a problem while simultaneously listening to the problem may cause leaders to miss a bigger issue or rush to a snap

The Rock

decision. Each problem demands its own special merit and therefore leaders must understand the merits of each problem. There may be one minor detail that makes it different from a similar problem. The ultimate goal is to fix one problem without creating a bigger problem. Effective listening can help reduce the chances of this happening.

I will use the same lieutenant discussed previously as an example. I must warn that the story is very heartbreaking, but it could have been much worse if not handled correctly. We had a soldier who was dealing with the painful issue of his spouse dying of cancer in a location that was far away from our current duty location. It would have been difficult for him to travel to be with her without a great deal of assistance from his leadership. When the soldier confronted his leader with the issue, the young officer simply shrugged it off as a personal problem. He wouldn't listen, and proceeded not to dedicate any additional time to listening. He had missed several small details of the problem and therefore jumped to a hasty conclusion: "This sounds like a personal problem" was the young officer's reply.

At this point the young soldier had no options and nowhere to turn, so he thought. However, he did make a last-ditch attempt to go to a higher level leader and this leader had the time to listen and fully understand the problem. It was only a matter of days before the soldier was on a plane and able to be with his spouse in her last dying days. The solution was complex and there were many others who had to be involved to implement the solution. Nevertheless, the bigger task was to simply hear the problem. This soldier's leader was willing to do neither.

Regrettably, the soldier's spouse did pass away, but at least her husband was able to be with her in her time of need. I highlight this particular story because, if the soldier had simply put his faith in what the young officer had told him, there is no telling what drastic measures the soldier would have taken if he were not a prudent person. Instead of one problem, this already complex and troubling situation could have easily led to many more problems. However, the soldier had faith that a leader in his chain of command would listen and he was right. It made all of the difference in the world to that one individual.

Listening effectively takes time and patience. If a leader is unwilling to commit the time or display the patience to listen to subordinates, two things are bound to happen: one is small problems will grow into larger ones, and two, no one will bring you their problems. Being labeled as someone who doesn't listen will foster problems coming to you in the worst form—late in the game or not at all.

Now, let us focus on those self-proclaimed good listeners that I like to refer to as "courtesy listeners." These individuals will generally give anyone the courtesy of listening to what someone has to say without absorbing what is being said. They pretend to hear what you say, but what they are really doing is processing their next point, with maybe a slight interest in what you are really trying to communicate. Their eventual goal is to maintain the lead, control the conversation or win an argument. You can easily recognize this when you are talking to this type of individual because he or she either begins talking as soon as the last word exits your mouth, or before you can get the last few words out of your mouth, they have already begun talking.

This, in military radio lingo, is what we would call being "stepped on." Hopefully, you remember the brief explanation of transmit and receive and the concept of not being able to do both on a military radio system. If you are talking and the person on the other end of the radio does not allow you to completely finish your transmission and begins to talk, your transmission is over-ridden and you are then the victim of being "stepped on."

Your transmission was cut short. The person on the other end did not have the benefit of hearing your full transmission. This happens just as easily during face-to-face conversations with courtesy listeners. The courtesy listeners are notorious for "stepping on" people. They are primed and ready to inject their counterpoint, or get their point across, without fully getting the gist of what the other person is trying to say.

If you are guilty of this, chances are you will quickly disengage those subordinates with whom you are talking. How can he relay what he is trying to say? He cannot fully get his point across. You are interrupting his train of thought, and most importantly, you are simply not listening! If on the other hand, you are attempting to offer feedback to a courtesy listener or to someone who doesn't listen well at all; all bets are off!

Leaders who want to be effective listeners can't be defensive when receiving feedback. Instead of listening to something that may benefit them, all energy is geared toward defending themselves.

Chris Musselwhite is the founder of Discovery Learning, an organization that focuses on human resource and organizational development. In an article titled,

"Self-Awareness and the Effective Leader," Musselwhite discusses the importance of leader's ability to receive feedback through effective listening:

> "When you are busy defending your actions, you miss what the person is trying to tell you. If on the other hand you listen and accept feedback without defending yourself, you are more likely to hear what you need to hear, increasing credibility with the person giving you the feedback and creating a trust bond that will enable them to continue providing useful feedback in the future."[31]

Nothing ruins the morale of an organization more than a leader or boss who simply won't listen. There has to be a desire on the part of the leader to listen. If he or she only wants to listen, to a chosen few in the organization, then chalk this up as a loss for the organization. Leader's may or may not realize that the result of ineffective listening is: 1) that problems stop coming your way, 2) the conversations that you purposefully try to generate are short-lived, and 3) surely no one in your organization will be willing to tell you when "the emperor has no clothes."

You should hope that your trusted circle has your back and will tell you when things are wrong because no one else will. As for problems not coming your way, I only have to refer to yet another great quote from Gen. Powell's *Leadership Secrets*: "The day Soldiers stop bringing you their problems is the day you have stopped leading them."[32] To deal with problems, you have to first hear the problem, then you have to understand to the problem, and only then can you deal with the problem.

The question is how good are your listening skills? A simple solution is to pause. When talking to others, be willing to pause and listen.

> **Soldier Quote: David Anderson,** "Listening/Complaining/Motivation: A leader utilizing a proper listening technique can understand the overall issue driving what's bothering the complaining soldier and its relevance to the mission. Once the bigger issue is derived, that leader can then apply the appropriate action to solve the problem or solve the complainer."

> **Soldier Quote: Eric Elton,** "Listening: For many years I never took the time to listen to anything or anybody. I heard them, but never really listened to what the words meant. When I finally started to listen to people, I realized I had missed out on a lot of wonderful lessons in life. Now when someone talks, I take the time to hear it all and *every time*, I learn something new."

Chapter 15

COMPLAINING

Pebbles: Complainers should have their own club . . . Oxygen Thief Association (OTA). When you complain, you are stealing valuable oxygen and producing hot air at the same time.

"There is no need in complaining because no one is going to listen anyway." This is a one of the many important quotes that I learned as a young officer.

Complaining and humans go together like peanut butter and jelly. Even the best of us have something to complain about on an occasional basis, even if we don't think it is a complaint. "Gas prices are too high." "It's too hot or cold outside." "The stock market is too low,"—general observations we all make from time to time and they appear to be just that, an observation. True, it may be a general observation, but for the most part, what are you willing to do about it? If the answer is nothing, then chalk it up as a complaint; you are

The Rock

simply complaining. Am I suggesting that people just stop making observations completely? Can you make a waterfall flow backward? Absolutely not!

True complainers are those who simply make it a daily habit to gripe, whine, or moan about something. You could give them a million dollar check and you would still be a dollar short of what they wanted. These folks are the ones who will drain the morale of your organization quicker than anything. Complainers are infectious and in most cases they operate in groups; "misery loves company" is a key motto for complainers. It is very hard to appease this group. In most cases you won't be able to appease them and in other cases you will spend a great deal of energy trying.

So what do you do? You learn to listen in a new way. You have to learn how to distinguish an illegitimate complaint from a legitimate complaint. Then you have to know how to deal with the complainer. This is a skill that I would argue we all have in some form or fashion.

The process of differentiating an illegitimate problem from a legitimate problem is necessary to prevent creating a larger or investing time in an irrelevant issue. There are a few questions you can ask the complainer that may help you distinguish the difference. What can you do about it? What are you willing to do about it? What have you done about it? Who else cares about this issue? If the answers you get are nothing and nobody . . . chalk it up as a gripe, whine, or illegitimate complaint.

Complainers are not quitters; they are very consistent and persistent. Another strategy is to try and find out what makes this complainer tick and in some cases you may not find an answer, although you may find a person who is not motivated, misinformed, misguided, or all of the above. Complainers also have another motto that goes "the squeaky wheel gets the grease." If you complain long and loud enough about something, you will eventually get the attention you were seeking.

This motto works well for those with legitimate issues who need an audience in which to air their grievance. Refer to the questions that I posed earlier to differentiate between legitimate and illegitimate complaints. My focus here is on the latter, those complaints that have the sole purpose of drawing and keeping attention on the complainer. They want to remain "squeaky" regardless of how much grease is applied. For some there are underlying issues that, if you can find the source, you may discover that all of the "squeakiness" was designed as a plea for help.

As an example, we had a new soldier and spouse team arrive at one of our subordinate units, and initially it appeared that their integration into the unit and military lifestyle was going very well. The little-known fact was that she was a perpetual complainer, possessed a strong personality, and a desire to be the center of attention. Army spouses are an integral part of the organization. Just as non-commissioned officers are considered the backbone of our formations, spouses serve as the backbone of their households and serve as a key part of the Army community. If mom/dad or the husband/wife is happy, everybody is happy! The soldier can function at work, is not distracted, and can give 100 percent effort to the tasks at hand. On the contrary, a misguided spouse can infect a unit single-handedly just as a single soldier can infect an organization if allowed to go unchecked.

Before long, it became obvious that this particular spouse possessed a voracious appetite and was never satisfied. At all the spouse gatherings, she had the most issues and even if things were corrected, it was just never good enough. On a few occasions, I was requested to help fix her issues, and as a battalion commander, I was three levels removed from the problem. Nonetheless, I was committed to lend my assistance because, regardless of your level in an organization, everyone is a problem-solver. Even with my help in getting her issues resolved, new ones would simply appear as fast as popcorn popping in a skillet. To make matters worse, she became infectious. It was easy to realize that gradually more and more spouses in that unit began to have problems.

In *Toxic People*, the author, Marsha Petrie Sue, describes these types of people as "whine and cheesers." She further expands by providing insights into things they complain about. "In some work environments, there are whine and cheeser parties about everything, including job duties, supervisors, colleagues, office supplies, the weather, and traffic—nothing is off limits for them."[33] This particular spouse was having "whine and cheeser" parties on a daily basis!

Her issues were not problems, but complaints that didn't have any real basis or truth. Unfortunately, she developed a following over time. Some followers were simply along for the ride because it was a free ride. What enabled her to get into this position was her strong personality. She possessed a personality that could have easily been used for good, but she preferred to utilize a positive trait in negative ways.

Once we analyzed this mini-epidemic, we were quick to realize that her following consisted of other spouses who were new to the military. They didn't know any better, but to them, she was the veteran after a period of time. So instead of one constant complainer, we had several, all within one unit. The other subordinate units did not have any spouse issues compared to this organization. The solution was simple in the overall sense.

I agreed to transfer her husband to what she believed was a "better" unit. There were some other factors bearing on this decision as well, but this was the key to allowing her to get what she really didn't want. To her advantage, she had a following of other spouses and she had several levels of a chain of command trying to cater to her every complaint. Life couldn't get any better for her. Uprooting herself from this was the least desirable option to her. Her hopes were to continue to receive endless concessions based on her endless complaints. In attempting to make a "power play" she really didn't believe anyone would make a transfer happen. This was a poor assumption on her part.

After the transfer took place, she found herself surrounded by a more experienced group of spouses, out of her comfort zone, and around a more mature group who could dispel her misguided complaints. What the transfer really satisfied was her need to have pressure taken off of her. As a young spouse attempting to take the reins as an informal leader, she was acting out for help. She didn't know how to use her talents in a positive way. An ability to complain and create dissent was what she assumed right-looked like. It took a while to figure out what may have appeared to be a simple problem in hindsight.

The reason I chose this example is because it demonstrates several things:

1. One person can have a tremendous negative affect on an organization, even if that person is at the lowest tier of the organization.
2. Dealing with complaints can consume a lot of organizational energy at multiple levels.

The Rock

3. Complainers can be infectious and a huge drain on organization morale.

Sometimes it is not enough to simply drown out a single complainer by not listening or by hastily categorizing a complaint as illegitimate. In complex situations like the one described, isolating the problem is a first step, and for the good of the organization, it is a good first step.

Some would call this "divide and conquer," but it was simply the effect of cutting away the bad part of an apple. Remove that apple, or at least remove the worm, because the rest of the apple will still be edible. Don't let a complainer ruin your organization.

Another way to deal with complainers is to use the "sand box." This is another favorite saying regarding complaining that I grew to embrace throughout my career. Think of this analogy with kids in mind. Do you ever remember how satisfying it was to play in a sandbox as a child? As kids, most of us would be content playing with the sand pail, shovel, and an assortment of other little odds and ends. You were at ease and in your own little world, only sharing it with a friend or two. Only another kid coming over to kick sand around or maybe even grab a toy or two could break this tranquility. Regardless, this would disturb the peace in that sandbox. The sand box represented your own little world with your own little boundary. Ultimately, the words "go play in your own sandbox!" would be the rally cry for the intruder to go back where she came from.

As soldiers or leaders, whenever you stepped too far out of the sandbox, someone would eventually remind you to stay in it—your area of expertise, your level of control, or your particular sphere of influence. This is another thing that gets complainers into trouble, as well as potentially taking the remainder of the organization along for the ride.

As a leader, you have to be aware of—areas of expertise, levels of control, and span of control within your organization. This will allow you to better understand these areas for individuals within your organization. Through promotions or increased responsibility, soldiers learn the Army one level of at a time. As you proceed up the organizational ladder, you gain a better understanding of roles within an organization and the interaction of your organization with others.

However, understanding gained from serving in a certain position is different than understanding that comes from observing others in that position. To illustrate, we all understand what our mail carrier is supposed to do based on observation (put our mail in our box, how hard is that?), but it doesn't necessarily mean that we could do it better. Unless we have had the experience of delivering mail, we are better to keep our critiques to ourselves. We think we understand what is supposed to happen, but then again, most of us haven't sat behind the wheel of a mail carrier truck either.

Complainers will often complain about things that are not necessarily in their sandbox. Not every complaint or issue is necessarily a bad thing, especially, if the complaint comes along with a good recommendation to fix the issue. Let's say that you find out about someone who is griping and whining about something that you are doing as leader. In more cases than not, this individual has probably not been afforded the opportunity to serve in your capacity, or so you would think. Go face-to-face with this individual and see what recommendations she would offer to fix the problem. If you get a half-baked or no answer, chalk it up as a complainer complaining. However, if you get a solid recommendation and something that makes you understand the issue that truly does pinpoint a problem, take it under advisement.

Listening to a potential complainer (one who is probably operating out of his sandbox) could prevent future complaints and distractions due to the fact that you let them air out their grievance. Individuals who constantly complain add little value to an organization, especially when they never offer solutions to a supposed problem. Rampant complaining can ruin many organizations and decrease overall productivity and morale. This could occur across multiple levels and it must be stopped. Left unchecked, complaining about the higher echelons of an organization has the ability to gain momentum and can be hard to reverse. As a leader, you have to be attuned to everyone's responsibilities and roles. Some individuals will have no perspective on the level of responsibility or decision-making required to perform in a certain capacity. This should prevent them from criticizing anything that a superior is doing. As a leader, you must have the courage to point out when others are completely out of their sandbox.

Complaining about something at some level is just human nature and there is also something to be said about levels of discontent in an organization. A little competitive friction in an organization can be healthy. You as a leader have to recognize the difference in the types of complaining that is occurring around you and what it is doing to your organization.

Those who provide viable solutions to complaints that they raise should be nurtured. The "whine-cheeser" complainers need to be isolated, or refocus them by getting them to remain in and focused on their own sandbox! Confront these types of complainers, because as a leader who knows and understands their level of control, responsibility, and sphere of influence, you can check to see how well they understand theirs. Get them to explain to you how perfect things are going in their part of the organization. If it becomes a challenge for them to give you direct answers, you will know that their sandbox is not the perfect place they think it is and that they themselves don't have all of their ducks in order.

The upside to this is that as a leader you can inspire them to focus that negative energy internally and challenge them to fix things in their own "sandbox." The downside is that this approach may not work and isolation may be in order to protect the rest of the organization, or in the most extreme cases, termination.

Playing in your own sandbox and helping others to stay within theirs is the ability to worry about those things that you can affect. If you can't affect how the boss is running a certain aspect of things, do not waste a lot of unnecessary energy complaining about it. Do what you can to ensure those under you are not affected by it.

The impact on motivation and inspiring others is the ability to raise the level of performance around you in order to create "healthy complainers" versus "whine and cheesers." It is healthier to solicit recommendations and allow them to be heard. This creates an environment where others become inspired to be creative. In essence you are turning complaints into recommendations with solutions.

Soldier Quote: David Guy, "I have always liked don't complain unless you have a solution, or at least guidance in the right direction."

Soldier Quote: Antonio Tricoche, "Complaining can be very annoying, but it's just as important as the rest it keeps the sanity in one's head when you are being tested physically and mentally. It's when people aren't complaining is when you worry."

Chapter 16

CHANGE

Pebbles: When change comes, don't fight it. You risk being blown away like a leaf in a tornado. Instead, embrace it. Don't let change affect you . . . you affect change!

Change can severely impact an individual's motivation level. Change is something that all our military service members are well accustomed to. We can change duty stations as frequently as once or twice a year in some cases. We can find ourselves in the United States one moment and Iraq, Afghanistan, Korea, or the Horn of Africa the next. For the most part, it is considered a necessity of the profession, and I for one enjoy this aspect of our profession. For many however, change can severely impact an individual in a negative manner.

The change that arguably brings the highest level of anxiety to Soldiers is the change of leadership. The reason I highlight leadership is because in most cases there is not a lot of research that can be done regarding your new

The Rock

leader. Even if you find a full biography and a life history, it cannot provide the insights that we are all curious about. Is this person sensible, reliable, intelligent, a good person, etc? It is this level of anxiety that unnecessarily affects one's motivation in a variety of ways.

There is a fear of the unknown that causes this anxiety. This one person could impact your motivation in one of three ways: good, bad, or not at all. It is generally natural to assume the worst and hope for the best. If 90 percent of the organization adopts this pessimistic outlook, the incoming leader is already working out of a deficit. No one knows what to expect, so the vast majority will expect the worst until proven wrong. The motivational bar is set low from the beginning.

This is not the incoming leader's fault. Individuals have set their motivation meters to low based on rumor, perception, or assumptions. The problem is that individuals don't recognize the affect they are having on their own motivation. The reason for this can vary widely. With this level of stress and anxiety rolling around in a person's head, it appears only natural that self-motivation will suffer.

You can't worry about change in a scenario such as this because it is coming whether you like it or not. If your self-motivation was high with the outgoing leader, what prevents you from keeping it that way, regardless of whom your leader is? This is what you control. Why give away your motivational steering wheel when no one asked you for it?

This is a tough question to answer. At times it can be a personal struggle to deal with change and keep your motivation level high. The impact of not doing this for yourself or those subordinate to you can have a tremendous impact on your organization's morale, regardless of size. As an individual, your daily outlook will be one of doom and gloom until either you leave or the leader leaves the organization.

The question simply becomes, how do we allow someone else that we don't even know to ruin our level of motivation? In layman's terms, how do we allow others to get into our heads? The answer is simple; the key word is "we". We do it to ourselves. You can't worry about what you can't control. If your source of motivation and inspiration walked away when the previous leader departed, I would recommend reevaluating what inspires and motivates you. The answer should be you!

Leaders must have the right attitude from the start in order to deal with change. A positive attitude will surely provide a foundation for high motivation. Trying to fake your way through change will eventually be apparent to those around you and more importantly to you.

As a case in point, leading an organization of any size in the Army is by all accounts a privilege and not a right. There are times when leaders are not afforded the opportunity to lead or command in a location of their choosing. On the face of it, this does not appear to be a big problem. However, there are those who have a problem with being placed in a privileged position that is not in a location of their liking.

If they never overcome the desire of their preference to be at one location as opposed to the other, their attitude will reflect this and so will their motivation.

Misery loves company, so for those in the organization who share the same outlook, their motivation will suffer as well. How can the leader inspire if he/she is not motivated? This is a selfish approach to being afforded a privilege, and it will cause the good of the organization to suffer. To illustrate, one of the senior leaders of my organization suffered from this problem and I or anyone who would listen heard about it almost daily. He couldn't focus on the tasks at hand or his responsibility to others because he was so concerned about where he should have been. As much as he tried to fake it, he couldn't come to grips with being somewhere that he thought he shouldn't have been.

Attempts to get him to see the positives in his current situation and realize the noticeable negative impact he was having on others in the organization fell on deaf ears. If I could have convinced him to change his attitude, things would have been better for him and the organization. He never overcame what was essentially a fight with his own mindset and level of motivation. His inability to accept change cost him a continued career.

Attitude is everything when it comes to motivating yourself and inspiring others. The only person who can ultimately affect this is you. Your circumstances, environment, or situation may impact your attitude and level of motivation, but only you can determine how big an impact you are going to allow it to make.

As a leader, if you cannot adapt your attitude and level of motivation based on change, it could have tremendous effects on the organization that you lead. Subordinates of any organization deserve the best from their leaders. The ability to adapt to change starts from within and can't be blamed on circumstances, location, or preference.

If you find yourself loathing a change that is about to occur, the only true option you have is to embrace it. You have to focus on any and all positive aspects of the impending change in order not to allow them to affect you personally. You cannot change what is about to happen. You can resolve to think of change as a positive and inspire others to do the same for their benefit and for the benefit of the organization.

> **Soldier Quote: Erik Choquette** on dealing with change, "With deliberate urgency. There's a Latin saying "Festina Lente" which means hurry slowly. I always remember this when it's time to show resiliency."
>
> **Soldier Quote: Vincent Mortara,** "Ride the wave and steer as efficiently and minimally as possible. Over time the steering will have changed your course completely."

Chapter 17

CONFIDENCE

Pebbles: When you walk out the door, think to yourself, *If it's me against the world today, the world is going to lose!*

One final element that produces motivation and the ability to inspire others is confidence! I view confidence similar to the way I view dreaming—when you dream, dream big! When you think about confidence, go big or go home!

When a challenge or task seems insurmountable, this is when you must boost yourself with a great deal of confidence. Confidence of this nature stems from competence. The more competent we feel about something, the more confident we are about doing it.

Your confidence has to be genuine. Others around you will sniff out a lack of confidence.

Confidence must not be confused with arrogance; there is a fine line between the two. Confidence is something that is contagious. You want to share it with others and you want others around you to be just as confident. When I stumbled across the following passage, I was shocked to find out that I wasn't the only one who felt this way about self-confidence and arrogance.

The former CEO of General Electric, Jack Welch, explains his view of confidence as:

> "There is a fine line between arrogance and self-confidence, but legitimate self-confidence is a winner. The true test of self-confidence is the courage to be open—to welcome change and new ideas regardless of their source. Self-confident people are not afraid to have their views challenged. They relish the intellectual combat that enriches ideas. They determine the ultimate openness of an organization and its ability to learn. You find these people by seeking out people who are comfortable in their own skin—people who like who they are and are never afraid to show it."[34]

Arrogance is the "fool's gold" of confidence. It looks like the real thing, appears to be real, but there is something missing—genuineness. Arrogant people are typically not genuine about anything except their own self-conceit. Pause for a second and think of a person that you view as the most arrogant person who you know. Now think about the characteristics of that person. I would be willing to bet that the laundry list goes something like this: very talkative, usually louder than the rest, preferred pronoun is "I", generally is a subject matter expert on virtually everything, and opinions of others are simply background noise to them. Is this close enough? If it doesn't exactly match your list, let's just say for argument's sake that I was in the ballpark.

Arrogance is about one thing: being self-centered. You can't transfer arrogance; it doesn't affect others in the positive way that confidence does. Arrogance often deteriorates environments; it causes malcontent, and is not healthy for any work or team environment. Arrogance in my opinion is usually the outward sign and display of a lack of confidence. What better way to cover up a lack of confidence? Pretend to be Superman! The key word here is "pretend."

You won't need to find kryptonite to deter this Superman or woman. Challenge them and you will see the obvious chinks in the armor. Do not allow yourself to be intimidated by the arrogant bully. Some will fall victim to this and think there isn't a chance to outsmart this otherwise sharp individual. Please do not misunderstand me at this point; there are some truly gifted individuals in the world who happen to be tremendously arrogant. After all, knowledge is power and abuse of power is sometimes a byproduct. I am not talking about those individuals; I am talking about those who are covering up low levels of confidence, and in some cases intellect, just for the sake of providing better control of their immediate surroundings.

Chris Musselwhite provides a good explanation of why this happens with leaders by asserting that "Many of us operate on the belief that we must appear as though we know everything all the time or else people will question our abilities, diminishing our effectiveness as leaders."[35] Musselwhite further expands on the impact on an organization when the leader professes to know everything or displays what I am referring to as arrogance:

> "It's easy to see how pretending to know everything when you don't can create situations that can be problematic for your entire organization. On the other hand, when you take responsibility for what you don't know, you benefit both yourself and your organization."[36]

If you are one of those arrogant people reading this now, you wouldn't even realize that this was a reflection of you. Why? Truly arrogant people (the type who are covering for a lack of confidence) also suffer from another problem—perception. These types of individuals lack self-awareness. Daniel Goleman defines self-awareness as "having a deep understanding of one's emotions, as well as one's strengths and limitations and one's values and motives."[37]

If you can observe this person in a non-threatening environment, one in which the organization is running well, egos are in balance, people generally work in harmony, etc., they still have to make it a point to be the "top rooster" in the hen house. The only way they can adapt is through intellectual bullying, abrasiveness, etc. They miss the point that their environment was non-threatening and fail to adapt to it because of a lack of self-awareness. Covering up a lack of confidence with arrogance only serves to do more to damage than good in any organization.

Unless this person owns up to his limitations, as suggested by Musselwhite, he misses the opportunity for self-improvement and so does the organization. In doing this, the opportunity to build genuine confidence

The Rock

by learning new things, embracing new ideas and people are never to be realized.

You can prevent yourself from falling victim to this by challenging this person's assumption, query his true knowledge level, or ask those pointed questions that get this person to elaborate on his latest line of BS. Bring him to your level if you think you are being perceived as being on a level lower than the "arrogant one." After all, how big a drag is this on your own morale and motivation to be around someone who is obviously "holier than thou?"

Don't allow this to affect you, and if anything, it should motivate you to want to brush up on a few extra things or broaden your curiosity to explore things that you may otherwise not know anything about. What could be more fun than "BSing" the "BSer?"

Confronting an arrogant bully can also be a huge confidence boost to know that you went head-to-head with Superman or woman and won. Before long, those around you are doing the same because without question they observed you do it. Don't take this lesson and supplant yourself as the new intellectual bully on the block; use it in positive ways to help others and those within your organization.

I often offer one word of advice to my subordinate leaders, which is to "study!" I offer this same advice to my kids, but with far less successful results. Kids will be kids and the last word they want to hear is the word "study."

Gen. Powell's *Leadership Secrets* alludes to this very concept. "Don't be afraid to challenge the pros even in their own backyard."[38] Never let your confidence be overshadowed to the point that your intellect is subverted along with it. In order to challenge the "experts," you need to prepare yourself, you need to 'study."

Even if you prefer to only concentrate on one particular thing, be the best at it and know the most about it. In *Drive: The Surprising Truth About What Motivates Us*, author Daniel H. Pink refers to this as "mastery." Pink outlines mastery, autonomy, and purpose as the three key things that motivate all of us. He describes mastery as "... a mindset. It requires the capacity to see our abilities, not as finite, but as infinitely improvable. Mastery is pain: It demands effort, grit, and deliberate practice."[39]

The bottom line is that you control the volume level of your confidence. One of the common references we use in the military is that competence breeds confidence. The more knowledgeable or competent you are about a particular area of subject matter, the more confident you become.

The bottom line is that you control your level of confidence and in doing so, control your level of motivation. What I suggested in the beginning was to get your confidence level so high that you feel invincible or as Daniel Pink asserts, you view your abilities as "infinitely improvable," this will surely boost your confidence. The amazing power of feeling good about yourself and knowing what you are capable of will make you feel as though you could conquer the world. That is the whole point! Another key difference with a confident person and the arrogant individual is that the arrogant one is not willing to share or change. Confident people share continuously, adjust to situations around them, and strive to make those around them better.

Soldier Quote: Vincent Mortara, "Confidence is the result of success, experience and wisdom. Confidence that comes from the mimicking of confidence is the saddest thing in leadership. Believe in yourself and what you are doing and like humility, love others and their success as well."

CONCLUSION

The Rock highlights the importance and demonstrates the impact of inspiration and motivation on leadership. Additionally, for those seeking ways to increase his/her level of self-motivation or inspire others, *The Rock* provides a few ideas designed to stimulate thought and provoke action toward sustainable self-motivation.

One of my key assertions is a defined purpose and an adequate level of direction is sufficient for any leader to guide an organization to success. However, without the power to motivate and inspire others, a leader is not fully maximizing the potential of that organization or the individuals within the organization. Motivation is an essential enabler of leadership.

There are many ways to motivate yourself and inspire others. In *The Rock*, I provided some of the tools and tricks of the trade that I have benefited from in my 22 years of service to the Army. I offered you my recipe for success: drive, confidence, change, listening, humility, me time, dreaming big, and investing.

Our ability to self-motivate determines everything we do and how well we do it. There are many things we as individuals can do to bolster and increase our level of self-motivation. Every organizational leader needs a "rock," a platform to rally the organization and allow everyone to be both seen and heard. Every individual needs a "rock," someone to help you see what you otherwise could not see—your ability to make a difference!

WORDS TO REMEMBER

Words to Remember is a collective combination of some of my most memorable quotes at the end of "close-out" formation briefings (memorable according to several soldiers who attended those briefs), as well as guidance I previously posted on Facebook.

I hope you enjoy them, share them. Most importantly, I encourage you to find your own way to inspire others and find the motivator in you!

MANCHU QUOTES

"At the end of every day
Look yourself in the mirror.
Do you see the person you can be?
Do you see the person you should be?
Do you see the Soldier we expect you to be?
If you don't know, look at the name on your left [U.S. Army is affixed to the left side of uniforms as they are worn]. If you don't know, look at the name on your right [last name is affixed to the right side of uniforms as they are worn]. Greatness rests in all of us. It is up to you to bring it out!"

Milford H. Beagle Jr.

"There is nothing average about our battalion.
There is nothing average about you.
This is where the strong survive and the weak stand on the sideline.
Don't be average; don't stand on anybody's sideline.
You didn't join the Army to be irrelevant.
You joined to make an impact.
Be proud of who you are; be proud of what you do!"

"Being a Manchu requires you to be better than other Soldiers, better than the average person.
Being a Manchu requires you to do something good or great for someone else—every day.
Anything less makes you irrelevant!
Be counted as a Soldier—Be counted as a Person—Be counted as a Manchu.
Be who you are supposed to be—not what anybody else wants you to be."

"Some people will tell you that it is not about you.
In this battalion, it is all about you.
You will make this battalion great.
You will make your company the best in the battalion.
You will make your platoon the best in the company.
You will impact someone's life by keeping this in mind:
It is all about you!
Without you, there is no US!"

"The life of a Manchu is a tough life.
It is tough because it is the price we pay to be good.
We will step up to the challenge when others won't.
We will always choose the hard right over the easy wrong.
We are driven because we are good.

The Rock

We are driven because of each other.
We are driven because we are Manchus!"

"PEBBLES"

Never Quit: When you receive that one piece of feedback that makes you want to say "screw it!" . . . that's Game Time! Fix the problem or issue and then serve it up like Venus [Williams]. Don't let someone's feedback knock you down . . . Get Up! Let's Go!

Your Destiny: Don't let "process" run your life because when you do, you forget about the "product" . . . you! You are the end product of your own life, so don't let the process of life create something that in the end you don't like. Control you destiny!

Motivation: What motivates us should motivate us forever . . . and what depresses us should only do so for a short time; ideally that is how it should be. Your biggest motivator is you; have you pumped yourself up today?

Be You: Never worry about those on the sidelines . . . run your race, play your game, do your thing! Noise from the sideline is just that . . . noise! Those on the sideline are simply afraid to play the game . . . now go get some!

Think Positive: Never underestimate yourself . . . let others do that for you. When it comes time to "show and prove", show it like a new car and prove it like a punch in the face (hard hitting). Get some!

Stress: Stress is not what others bring to you; it is what you bring on yourself . . . if you let others penetrate the safest vault in the world (your mind). Relook at your security system . . . don't let others stress you! Don't give others your combination to your vault unless you want to receive many stress deposits.

The Truth Hurts: Don't run from the truth; it hurts when it catches up to you (like a punch in the face from Manny Pacquiao; like the saying the "truth hurts") . . . simply face it (meaning find the good in the truth that is coming at you). The blows are a lot less painful and you are better for it. So next time don't get mad when you hear the truth . . . simply stick and move!

ACKNOWLEDGEMENTS

Throughout my life, I have had a very supporting and loving family. None of them ever placed limits on me or shattered what I wanted to achieve in life, even if I didn't know myself. I lived all of my childhood and most of my adult life around my grandparents. (May they all rest in peace.) I would like to thank many of my family members: Ralph and Gladys Dawkins, John and Carrie Beagle, Milford Sr. and Anna Beagle, Annie Mae Thomas, John and Delphine Leake, Chris Dawkins, Gloria Merrill, Robert and Madge Byrd, Henry and Emma Dawkins, CSM (ret) Edward Jones Sr. and Reverend Bernice Parker-Jones, Edward, Regina and Zachary Jones, Herschel and Linda Beagle, Jimmie and Jannie Mae Beagle, Al and Angie Beagle, James and Renee McKissick.

I would like to acknowledge some of the leaders who have proven to be sources of motivation for me for more than 22 years. I have not seen some of them for as many years, but the experience of being around them and learning from them was truly inspirational on every occasion. To my former leaders, current mentors and dear friends, I would like to thank you for your lifetime of commitment to soldiers, and families: LTC (ret.) John S. Lowe, COL (ret.) Stan Clemmons, LTG John W. Morgan, MG Michael T. Harrison, Sr., COL (ret.) Greg Gardner, COL (ret.) Peter Cassi, MG Gary S. Patton, BG Jeffrey Bannister, BG (ret) Thomas M. Jordan, MG Walter Golden, COL Joseph Southcott, COL Thomas and Karen Graves, and Mr. and Mrs. Joseph Bonnet, CSM Raul and Bobbi Huerta. Thank you all.

There are too many peers and soldiers alike who I would like to thank, but there are many of you who have impacted my life and career. Thank you.

Lastly, I would like to thank the Soldiers of 2nd Battalion, 9th Infantry Regiment (Manchu); without the soldiers of this unit as my motivation, *The Rock* would have never been possible. Thank you for bringing out the motivator in me.

NOTES

1. U.S. Department of The Army, *Army Leadership: Competent, Confident, and Agile*, Field Manual 6-22, (Washington, DC: U.S. Department of the Army), October 2006, p. 1-2
2. Ibid., p. 1-2
3. William H. Montogomery III, "Beyond Words: Leader Self-Awareness and Interpersonal Skills", U.S. Army War College: Carlisle Barracks, PA, 2007, p. 11
4. The Holy Bible, (Nashville, TN: Thomas Nelson Inc.), 1984, p. 256
5. Oren Harari, *The Leadership Secrets of Colin Powell*, 1st Ed., (New York, NY: McGraw Hill), 2002, p. 133
6. Nate Allen and Tony Burgess, *Taking the Guidon*, 1st Ed., (DE: Center for Company Level Leadership), p. 136
7. Marsha Petrie Sue, *Toxic People: Decontaminate Difficult People At Work Without Using Weapons or Duct Tape*, (Hoboken, NJ: John Wiley and Sons, Inc.), 2007, p. 175
8. Ibid., p.1-3
9. Colonel (Retired) Dandridge M. (Mike) Malone, *Small Unit Leadership*, (Novaton, CA: Presidio Press), 1983, p.147
10. John C. Maxwell, *Talent is Never Enough*: Discover The Choices That Will Take You Beyond Your Talent, (Nashville, TN: Thomas Nelson Inc.), 2007, p.196

[11] Gregory Gardner, "*Secrets to Success*" from NetApp's Greg Gardner: Personal is Memorable, email message to author, October 26, 2011

[12] Ibid.

[13] Ibid.

[14] Gardner

[15] Jon Gordon, *The Energy Bus: 10 Rules to Fuel Your Life, Work, and Team with Positive Energy*, (Hoboken, NJ: John Wiley and Sons, Inc.), 2007, p. 152

[16] Ibid., p. 152

[17] Discovery Channel. "Surviving the Cut". DiscoveryChannelStore.com. Retrieved 18 April 2011; http://en.wikipedia.org/wiki/Ranger_School, accessed November 12, 2011

[18] Daniel H. Pink, <u>Drive</u>: *The Surprising Truth About What Motivates Us*, (New York: Riverhead Books), 2009, pp. 111-128

[19] Ibid.

[20] Ibid.

[21] Ibid.

[22] Ibid.

[23] Ibid.

[24] Daniel Goleman, *Emotional Intelligence*, (New York: Bantam Books), 1995, p. 46.

[25] James M. Kouzes and Barry Z. Posner, *The Leadership Challenge*, (San Francisco: Jossey-Bass), 2002, pp. 85-86

[26] Ibid., Harari, *The Leadership Secrets of Colin Powell*, p. 256

[27] Robert W. Eichinger and Michael M. Lombardo, "*The 6 Qs of Leadership*," Lominger in Focus, 2006, p. 12

[28] Michael Lombardo and Cynthia McCauley, The Dynamics of Management Derailment, Technical Report Number 34, (Greensboro, NC: Center for Creative Leadership), 1988

29 Ibid., Montogomery, "Beyond Words: Leader Self-Awareness and Interpersonal Skills", p. 11

30 Anthony J. Rucci, "What the Best Business Leaders Do Best," in Rob Silzer, ed., The 21st Century Executive: Innovative Practices for Building Leadership at the Top, (San Francisco: Jossey-Bass), 2002, p. 35

31 Chris Musselwhite, "Self Awareness and the Effective Leader," 1 October, 2007, http://www.inc.com/resources/leadership/articles/20071001/musselwhite.html?utm (accessed 10 October 2011)

32 Ibid., Harai, *The Leadership Secrets of Colin Powell*, p. 256

33 Sue, *Toxic People: Decontaminate Difficult People At Work Without Using Weapons or Duct Tape*, p. 70

34 Jack Welch, *Straight From the Gut*, (New York: Warner Books), p. 384

35 Ibid, Musselwhite, "Self Awareness and the Effective Leader"

36 Ibid.

37 Ibid., Goleman, *Emotional Intelligence*, p. 46.

38 Ibid., Oren Harari, *The Leadership Secrets of Colin Powell*, p. 256

39 Ibid., Daniel H. Pink, *Drive: The Surprising Truth About What Motivates Us*, p. 56

CPSIA information can be obtained
at www.ICGtesting.com
Printed in the USA
LVHW031612101218
599930LV00001B/34/P